THE GREAT STONE CIRCLE

Heather Maxwell

PublishAmerica
Baltimore

Hardcover 978-1-4512-7793-7
Softcover 978-1-4512-7794-4
PUBLISHED BY PUBLISHAMERICA, LLLP
www.publishamerica.com
Baltimore

Printed in the United States of America

Dedication

PROLOGUE

A sea of whirling colors and bright light was all the old Indian could see as he struggled to breathe. With a wheezing thick cough and a hard swallow, his breath started to come a little easier. Echata thought to himself; "My head feels so heavy, I have felt a lot of different pains in my life, but what is that strange cold ache in the middle of my back? Could I be lying on a sharp stone?" He squirmed back and forth grinding his shoulders into the dry hard earth, trying to find the relief that somehow kept evading him.

As Echata's vision started to clear, he wearily turned his head and looked back towards the woods. Suddenly his eyes caught movement in the distance, and there he saw waddling away was the sow black bear that had just attacked him. Slowly Echata began to realize what had happened to him. He mumbled to himself; "That old sow must have some cubs somewhere, I must have looked like an intruder to her!"

Echata then tried to sit up, when a searing hot pain raced across his abdomen, causing him to cry out in agony and flop like a rag doll thrown to the ground. Perspiration had started to bead upon his trembling upper lip as he sputtered; "Wh wh what is that!?" Carefully he reached down and slid his blood-soaked deerskin shirt away from his body. Panic and weakness raced through him as his red sticky fingers began to feel the large jagged hole that had been ripped into his belly. His mind began reeling with horrifying thoughts. Stammering out loud he Yelled; "I must get back! For who will take care of my people!?"

Echata tried with all his might to roll over, but his legs wouldn't move. They felt strange and heavy like they weren't really his. After several struggling futile attempts, Try as he might, he just couldn't make his lower half move. His legs just laid there like heavily rooted fallen trees. He was even unable to wiggle his toe.

Exhausted he laid there a crumpled bloody heap, staring at the darkening sky. Agony began filling his mind when he realized that his back must also be broken.

Echata's concern was not so much for himself, but for his people. For so many of them depended upon him. He mournfully let out a low guttural growl and groaned; "There is so much I should have done long ago! And for this, my people will suffer."

Mustering up what little strength he had left, he pushed himself up as high as he could, and shouted; "Brother Wind!

Hand messenger of The Great Spirit! I am Echata-Quai-Atoke! I await your coming!"

He then fell to the ground expelling the last of his strength. His mind began to wander as he felt his life slowly ebbing away. Mixed thoughts summoned his earliest childhood memories, but his very last one he strained hard to see, he only wished to recapture the image of his mother's face. Suddenly, he was swept away into another reality as he began to relive his life's memories…

PART 1
Echata-Quai-Atoke

Many life times ago, in the Pacific Northwest, far to the northeast of an area that would some day become Seattle; Is a small circular range of mountains with a low-lying valley in the interior. This valley is called "Nai-Pee-Ah" which in the English tongue means, "abundant life." The inhabitants who live there, the "Chono-Oo-Ee-Pay B-Doda" (Children Of The Great Spirit) named the valley this due to the lush green pastures & the bountiful mountain lake that is full of fish and cool snowy mountain water.

Twelve generations of the Chono-Oo-Ee-Pay B-Doda have passed since the construction effort began on The Great Stone Circle. As the completion draws near, all the village inhabitants await the birth of "The promised one." A boy child, who is to be born to a man named "E-Ish Tamoe" (Seventh-Seer) & his wife, "Nosh-Nay-Ya Oo-Ma-Hayo" (Lake Fishing Woman.) Their child was "The one who was to come." This had been foretold of and handed down through the tribal elders. He is to be the tribe's medicine man and the most important of all, the guardian of The Great Stone Circle.

The day of his birth, Lake Fishing Woman brought their first born son to her husband, and with over whelming love, she placed the child in his arms. Seventh-Seer said; "This brings me much joy my life love, my spirit is soaring high like the red tailed hawk upon the wind. So this is what I shall name our son, "Echata-Quai-Atoke" (Joy Of The Soaring Hawk.) The boy's path in life had already been chosen and carefully planned out before he was born. All of the customs of the people were to be divinely instituted, and scrupulously adhered to. Echata was to be trained in the natural way; to keep in close contact with the natural world. In this way, he would find himself and become conscious of his relationship to all life. For unlike other children, he was never to learn the way of the warrior or how to use weapons. For this only condoned the act of shedding blood. This action was expressly forbidden to him. Because he was never to take a life, not even that of an animal. In this way the spiritual world would then be real to him, allowing the splendor of all lives that belong to The Great Spirit to stand out above all else.

Echata was taught by both example and instruction, but with the emphasis on example as true politeness towards his people was defined by his actions and not his words. He was not to speak while others were speaking, or pass between the fire and an elder or visitor, for this was considered a thoughtless action by anyone, let alone a child. He was to respect the adults, especially the old ones. He was not allowed to join in their discussions, or directly address them. Only by way of relationship or some kind of title was he allowed to use, instead of their given name. This is how he showed respect.

This bright and gentle child who seemed to know by instinct his peoples way of life, grew to the point of understanding when he was about 8 winters old. He was to be kept ever before the public eye. Not a step in his development was over looked as an excuse to bring it before the people by giving a feast in his honor. Thus his progress was known to the whole tribe as to a larger family, and he would grow with a sense of reputation to sustain.

During such feasts, his parents often gave so generously to the needy that they almost impoverished themselves, thereby setting an example to Echata that self denial is for the public good. Not only did this show him that big heartedness, generosity and courage were the qualifications of a public servant, it taught him self worth as well. The tribe believed that enlisting him early in public service would develop a wholesome ambition for the honor of tribal leader.

The long winter evenings are considered the proper time for the learning of those traditions that have their roots in the past and lead back to the source of all things. And since the subjects lay half in the shadow of mystery, they have to be taken up at night, the proper realm of mysticism.

Through the telling of these tales, the parents inspire love of heroes, pride of ancestry and devotion to the people. But these tales do more than enlarge the mind and stimulate the imagination. They furnish the best of memory training, as Echata is required to remember and repeat them one by one. These methods of transmitting from father to son an account of all things is faithfully preserved, so that succeeding generations are acquainted with what has passed. In doing things this way, it may not be forgotten.

At the end of each long winter day, when Echata and his family had settled in their lodge for the night, they would gather around the fire in anticipation of beginning their songs of praise to honor The Great Spirit. After this, Echata's Father would recite the stories of tribal history and tradition. Followed by the greatest undertaking of his people, the construction of The Great Stone Circle.

Echata absorbed the words as they began to take on a life of their own. The rhythms in which they were spoken and chanted opened a floodgate of images and thoughts so he could feel the very heartbeat and sense the life experiences that they contained. To Echata, it was like listening to the elders ceremonial drums that wove a hypnotic spell from the passion in which they were beaten. The songs of the spirits of great men who with their words, found love, faith, and the healing of their hearts as they entertain the minds of the listeners.

Seventh Seer began his recitation this way;
Long ago when our people were few and our tribal strength was uncertain, we gathered In this valley. Our leader "Chue-Nue Quai-Ta" (Raising Prayer Smoke) said;"This is a good place, full of game and surrounded by mountains to protect us. It is like being in the open hand of The Great Spirit, surely we will be blessed."

Several winters had passed and one day Raising-Prayer-Smoke found himself in a waking dream. He was shown by The Great Spirit the way to perform a 7-day purification ceremony. He was told to gather 6 of his wisest men and perform this ceremony.

The ancient purification ceremony is to be performed totally nude. It has to do with facing The Great Spirit the way you came into this world. And in preparation, 3 days before you begin and all during the purification, no meat is to be eaten. Only fruit, herb and plant matter, for if you consume flesh, you carry the smell of death with in you.

To start the ceremony, you begin by lighting the sacred fire. This fire represents mans struggle for survival, it must not be allowed to go out until the ceremony is over. For the next seven days, from dawn until dusk, special tribute of honor respect and thankfulness is given to the following;

The first day; is mother earth—The womb of life, where all physical life began.

The second day; is father sky—Everlasting star filled heavens, the dominion of The Great Spirit.

The Third day; is the sun—Illumination, truth, the cycle of life and growth.

The Fourth day; is the moon—Sister to the sun, the time keeper, and the watchful eye of night.

The Fifth day; is the wind—Hand messenger of The Great Spirit, a reminder that he is always close.

Sixth day; is water—Bringer of life, and born of water, without It nothing lives.

The Seventh day; is all plant life—Man's partner and provider in life, the breast of mother earth. This is followed by a three day fast while waiting for insight from The Great Spirit.

Raising-prayer-smoke selected his men and began to perform the ceremony. And just as it was promised, The Great Spirit moved upon them and gave guidance to each of the men, a special insight all his own. But none would benefit from it unless they were united as one; and as this was done, they received the vision of The Great Stone Circle.

The following spring when the ice melted and the trees put forth new life, the seven men preformed the Ceremony again, and they received a new insight; that the next day, the seven men were to gather their things and travel east to sacred mountain. Where at it's base is an entrance to a large cavern. This is where they were told to build The Great Stone Circle.

Many winters passed and the building continued until each man grew too old to work. And as this happened, each man would train his first-born son to take his place. It has been this way for 12 life times, and we are descendants of the very first builders."

Tribal history and tradition reciting was always Echata's favorite time of day. For learning about his people was the single most important thing he could ever do. And even from his young age, Echata knew his importance in life was determined by the well being and care of his fellow villagers.

He was taught to seek the help of his spirit guides whenever he was in need or in doubt of his abilities. But being such a new spirit himself, this was a lifetime spiritual quest. Not an ability to be obtained and used as a child. So needless to say as Echata grew older; His seemingly simplistic life began to change. No other had come before him, so the village inhabitants had no way of knowing that Echata's position in life would extract a heavy toll. As unforeseen conditions would forge him into the man he would someday become.

When Echata was about 10 winters old, it became increasingly harder for him to fit in with the other children. Especially when all the other boys wanted to be like their fathers and make weapons of wood like spears and clubs and pretend to make the hunt. When they did this, it left Echata out of the group. It wasn't long before they started making fun of him by telling him to go help the women. They would say; "You'll never be a true man or a defender of the tribe."

This tore at his heart and hurt him deeply. As Echata always thought of his people first. He just couldn't understand why they wouldn't accept him for who he was to become. Or why they needed to make fun of him. As far as he was concerned, they were the same. But they would often follow him chanting, "girl child, girl child girl child" this did nothing but drive Echata into seclusion where he delt with the teasing on his own. So he thought…One day as Echata's mother was checking her fish traps at the edge of the lake, she overheard sounds of whimpering coming from a patch of tall reeds. She drew closer to investigate, and there she found Echata; hiding in the reeds crying. "My son, what troubles you so?"

Echata looked into his mothers soft brown eyes and said;

"The other boys, they call me girl child just because I won't make weapons or play the hunt. I tell them it is not the way for me, but they won't listen. They scoff at me and walk away…I will always be alone…won't I mother?"

Cradling me in her arms, she smoothed my wet hair away from my face and said;

"Echata, life can seem hard when you are so very young. Do not let the other boys teasing cause you to be unhappy. They are young themselves and they know not what they do. One day, those same boys will be coming to you for guidance. For now, try to forget their foolishness and come and help me while I pull up the net."

"Mother! What if the other children see me do this?"

Letting out a soft sigh, mother said;

"Echata, why would you care what they think, they have already teased you, what harm will it do if you hold my sack for me?"

"Nothing I guess."

Dutifully I followed my mother and watched as she tossed a bag filled with walnut husks into the lake and slowly pull the net to the surface. The fish would squirm to and fro showing their multi faceted colors that glistened in the exposed sunlight on their slick silvery skin. She would then grab the line that was attached to the bag and pull it back out. The fish would be momentarily stunned from the tannic acid, thus allowing her to pick them up with ease and club them once in the head and toss them into her open sack.

Maybe it was because I never had to kill something in order to fill my always hungry stomach. But I felt a pang of sadness as I watched the net filled with dozens of fish fighting for life as the lake water oozed out of the small holes and slowly suffocated them. Somehow I identified with these fish, for at times I felt like I was slowly being ensnared.

Early on I found that my only defense was to shield myself with arrogance. This distanced me from the other children even more. It created a great loneliness and only added to the struggle of my situation. I slowly began spending more and more time away from the village, finding solace in the creatures of the forest. These animals are made by The Great Spirit just as I am.

That makes them my brothers and my sisters. They never make fun of me and they accept me for who I am. They shall be my tribe, and I of theirs. This small act, gave me happiness once again.

Two of my favorite animals were the otter who was always up for play; and the other, a fat slow moving groundhog that lived near the lake. This pudgy little fellow found a soft spot in my heart. I felt a kinship to him, for like him; he could not change who he was born to be. And his only defense against predators was to hide away in his neatly concealed burrow.

One of the pleasures I had with him was to take the tender insides of the tall cattail plant, and leave them as food offerings outside of his burrow. I would then wait close by and watch and soon the groundhog would emerge. While I watched this pudgy fellow devour his treat, I would often snack on one of my mothers pemmican bars. Occasionally I would pick out some of the dried black berries and toss them over in his direction.

Seeing his puzzled expression as he sniffed the berries, then disdainfully reject them always made me laugh. I knew he wouldn't like the smell of them; because they were dipped in melted bear fat so they would cling to the dried meat. Sharing a simple snack with someone other than my parents, somehow didn't make me feel so alone.

Amidst all of my great loneliness and pain, there was one boy that seemed to get great pleasure out of tormenting and being cruel to me. This boy's given name was "Mastado-Cha" Which, the closest interpretation of this is "Dark Morning", which seemed to fit his personality. He received this name from his father, when his mother died bringing him into this world.

Dark Morning was an exceptionally large child with a mass of long thick tangled black hair. With dark eyes that appeared too small for his face and a long slightly crooked nose from a battle of wills with a low hanging branch; He looked every bit the part of what his name represented, a Dark Morning.

He had a horribly cruel nature. So without a mother's guidance to keep him in check, he quickly became a prominent bully with a few followers. The other boys followed Dark-Morning not because they wanted to, but because this was the safest position to be in. The boys felt that being a follower was much easier than becoming one his numerous victims of harassment.

As fate would have it, Dark Morning became a continual nightmarish presence in my early life. And I spent my days trying to avoid his onslaught of ridicule and cruelty.

One afternoon, I heard a great disturbance going on outside my lodge. When I went out to investigate, what I saw made me weak in the knees and filled me with rage. There stood Dark Morning wearing an evil sadistic grin. He started laughing as he presented my groundhog to me hanging off the end of a wooden spear.

"Look what I'm having for dinner you "Ma-Chono—Toe-Ah" (Mud Frog) You cannot hide from me! I followed you to your secret place of hiding, and saw you feed this fat thing. Maybe I'll use his skin to make a ball and kick it around the village! What are you going to do to stop me?!"

Fighting back the tears, I quivered with rage. All I could do is slowly turn around and go back inside my lodge. I knew I had no chance of doing anything to Dark-Morning. For I had countless memories of others who had tried and were beaten to the ground.

I grabbed my knees and started rocking back and forth like I did as a child with a belly ache. I was trying hard to control the fires of rage that engulfed me while I heard Dark Morning shouting with glee and the steady "thump, thump, thump" as he kicked my little friend around like a ball. Silently I prayed and sang my songs of praise to The Great Spirit, asking him to take away my pain and ease the burning fire within me.

Later that afternoon, my mother came home and found me. I was still fuming with uncontrolled rage when she softly said;

"I have heard what Dark Morning has done, and I am glad you did not try to fight him. I fear you would have been hurt."

I couldn't disguise my scornful tone;

"That piece of dung Deserves to die!"

"Please don't say such things Echata, he is just a confused child, alone in this world. In his mind he is lost and knows not what to do. So to feel strong, he tries to control others. And to ease his own pain, he inflicts it on anyone he can."

"You see, his father blames him for his mother's death. And has little to do with him. He has no other living family and life in this world has been hard for him."

"I know it is difficult for you to understand right now, and in the seasons to come, a lot of things may not make much sense. But as you grow into a man, things will soon become clear."

"Mother, I just don't understand why I should have to endure things that hurt me so much."

"My child, if there was no hurt in this world, how would we know all the goodness that life brings? It takes both feelings, and many more, to become whole. Just as we need the harsh cold winter snow, we also need the warm summer rain. It is only a cycle my son, and it always turns."

"When I was a small girl, my father told me that "when you begin great work, you can't expect to finish it all at once." So you need to press on and let nothing discourage you until you have finished what you've begun. But I assure you, you will move on from this my son. And even though the winds may blow strong in your face; go forward and never turn back. You must not take notice of this or that. But hear me my son when I speak to you; and take it to heart, for you may always depend on what I say shall be true."

My mother was always trying to help me understand why my life was so difficult. I never realized how much I depended upon her until a few days later, when the hand of fate asserted itself once again with another life changing tragedy.

One early morning while I was memorizing the concoctions of sweet and dry herbs procured for the sick, My father called to me;

"Go down to the lake and see if your mother needs some help Echata, she has been gone longer than usual."

"Yes father!"

I ran down to the lake eagerly looking for my mother, I searched through the tall wet reeds & cattails that surrounded the big lakes edge.

my moccasins were sinking deep into the wet balmy mud and making funny squishing noises with every step. I called for my Mother time and time again but received no answer.

"Mother, are you there?" "Where are you Mother?"

I wanted to run around the lake edge as fast as I could, but my legs would sink up to my knees in the wet pungent earth, making it almost impossible to move quick. The tall reeds weren't allowing me to see anything very far, as this time of year they were almost as tall as I.

Clouds of gnats and Insects were swarming in big circular moving shapes in the early morning sun, causing my eyes to tear and my nose to run as I dredged through the reeds; I was even inhaling them. I spit them out hastily and ignored it. My only care was to find my mother.

As I came up over a small rise next to a group of willow saplings, lying there at the water's edge was my mother's fish sack. It appeared as if it had been thrown from a great distance. I slowly walked over to her sack, and grasped it and began picking up the newly caught fish that were strewn around. Calling her name aloud I still didn't get a response.

A growing sense of urgency and instinctively knowing that something was horribly wrong; I became engulfed in panic, and turned to run back to the lodge to get my father.

My lungs burned and my thighs ached but I kept running, faster and faster until I could see my home in the distance.

I started screaming for my father even before I reached our lodge.

"Father, Father! Mother is not at the lake, I cannot find her. Her fish sack was thrown to the ground and she was no where near it! Please father, you must hurry to find her!"

My father felt the fear in my voice, and knew I was right.

"Stay here! I will be back!"

Even he couldn't keep his fear and apprehension from his voice. My father ran out of the lodge with such haste, without even pulling on his deerskin moccasins. I could hear him yelling at the others to gather and help him look for my mother.

After what seemed like hours, I heard people crying outside. I started to go investigate, when my father appeared in front of me at the opening of our lodge. His face was sullen and grief stricken. He gathered me in his strong arms and with his jaw tight and teeth clenched, in a quiet quivering voice, said;

"Boy, we have found your mother…she has gone on to the other world."

I slid from my father's arms as I heard a weird mewling sound, almost that of a new born child, I then collapsed onto the floor and broke into uncontrollable sobbing.

Engulfed with grief, my father then turned and blindly stumbled out of our lodge, leaving me to deal with my pain on my own.

When my convulsions stopped, and my tears had run dry; I went to my find father. He was sitting alone by the lake, in front of a deserted fire pit. He was holding my mothers carved deer antler necklace she had been wearing. And with a voice that didn't sound like my own, I slowly started to speak absently to his turned back. As I could tell he did not want me to see his face.

"Father, I feel strangely numb all over...and I have no more tears inside me...Is it real?...Is mother really gone?... what happened to her?"

"We really couldn't tell what happened. Only that she had a wound on the back of her head...we found her deep underwater, tangled in the mangled lake reeds. Your mother's brother, "Te-See Kan-Ah" (Talks Quiet) will be the one to help me carry her to Sacred Mountain and place her in the cave of Resting Souls. Tomorrow when he is done preparing the elk robe to wrap her in, we will stop by here on the way to the cave so you can tell her good-bye."

With that being said, and without so much as an acknowledgement that I was still standing there, my father stopped talking and continued turning my mother's necklace over and over again in his fingers. I knew he had nothing else to say.

Slowly I fumbled my way back to our lodge. Alone and distraught, I longed to feel my mother's presence once again. And the only thing I could do to console myself was to lay down on the elk skin furs that she and my father used for a bed.

I pressed my nose deep into the fur and hungrily inhaled my mothers lingering scent of mixed herbs and dried berries that clung to the soft silkiness that enveloped my dirty tear stained face.

As I lay there, I had no sense of passing time. Only that the suns shadow had long since passed over before I felt strong enough that I could emerge from the self inflicted torture that I had cocooned my self in.

When I slowly merged myself back into reality, I found that my father had not returned to our lodge. Growing fearful that I would lose him also, I decided to go and look for him. Stepping out in to the darkness, I felt a strange and unwelcome chill. It crept up my spine and shot down my arms like the bright light that comes from the sky after a spring rain. I shrugged it off and went about my search.

My first stop was the central meeting lodge. I thought maybe our tribal elders had gathered with my father for prayer. But I soon discovered this was not so. The smoldering pit was unattended and there was only heavy imprints left in the dirt from the many feet that had danced in worship around what was once a blazing fire.

Realizing that I had no other place to look, I turned and was making my way back to our lodge when my ears picked up on a soft song being sang somewhere deep in the darkness. I don't know why I didn't hear it sooner, for as I drew closer, the song became clearer and clearer as it traveled effortlessly upon the wind.

Ever so slowly my body began to sway back and forth in time with the soft mumbled song being sung in the distance. I didn't even know I had stopped walking. My flesh rippled with bumps, and my eyes closed, and for the first time that day, I started to feel peace. It filled my body with a slow moving warmth, the same way the sun does when I lay in its bright glow on a hot summer day.

Within moments the song vanished like a wisp of smoke in the late night breeze and my melancholy state took over once again. I guess that is how my life is going to be, only bright moments of pleasure intermingled in a lifetime of pain.

Feeling more saddened than I had before, I bowed my head and hunched my shoulders and began walking again. I had no destination in mind, and felt as though my feet were carrying me into the unknown. I was only vaguely aware of the journey I was on, and it wasn't long before I was standing at the tree lined base of sacred mountain. My stomach began churning with the thought of my beautiful mother being carried up the rock lined path and placed in the cave that I have always been so afraid of.

The Children of The Great Spirit named this cave "Oo-Eee-Pay Nay-Nah" (Resting Souls.) But I have never called it by this name. I call it, "Oo-Eee-Pay Sho Nah-Nay-Nah" (Whispering Souls) as it has never sounded like they were resting to me.

As far back as I can remember; I have always been able to hear my ancestors whispering coming from the cave. I know not what they say, as it sounds as though a great many are speaking at once. When I was a small child, I would often hear my name being called from somewhere within the cave, and this would frighten me. I knew that as of late, no one had passed on to the other world, and that there should be no living beings inside the cave. But yet, I was always being summoned by someone or some thing.

When I spoke to my mother about the voices I heard, she would only smile and remind me that I was "the one who was to come" and that my ancestors were very happy I was finally here, and they only wished to say hello. For many lifetimes had to pass before I was to arrive. Remembering this only saddened me further as I never thought of my mother being part of the inevitable future that all of us must some day face, as we pass from this world into the next.

The sun cresting upon the mountains & turning the dimly lit charcoal colored sky into the coming dawn brought me out of my trance like state. I knew that I must get back home, for soon my uncle would be bringing mother to me so that I could say good bye.

Off in the distance I could already hear the slow methodical beat of our tribal elders prayer drums waiting to lead my mothers body in her spirit walk that would start at our lodge, and then weave through the center of our village with it eventually ending at her body's final resting place; The dreaded cave of whispering souls.

The drums were beaten to "awaken our ancestors and let them know someone had begun their journey home." And once this started, I knew I wouldn't have much time with mother, so I forced myself to run; My stumbling impeded my progress, but I eventually made it.

My mother's body wrapped in an elk skin blanket was all I could see when I rounded the edge of our lodge. The women of the village had placed rows of wild flowers all around my mother's small form, intermingled with the long vines from the willow tree that was only 10 paces from my home.

At that moment, I wanted to climb inside the blanket with her, for I felt as though I was already dead. I don't know how long I had been standing there, but my father's gentle voice nudged me out of my thoughts.

"Echata, it is time for your mother's walk, please say your goodbye's."

Shakily, I walked up to my mother. I looked at the shape of her tiny feet under the blanket. Slowly I reached out my trembling hand and placed it at the tip of her toe and slid it over her foot and up to her hand and over her shoulder to rest on her shielded delicate face.

My mouth could form no words, and my voice would find no sound within me. For at that moment, there were no words to convey my loss. The only goodbye I could give were the salty tears that had pooled in my eyes and slid off my cheeks and dropped to the earth. Helplessly I watched, as father and uncle carried her off into the distance.

I was unaware of my surroundings as people slowly filed past me. Everything seemed to be a blur. I wanted to turn and run to find a place to hide, but Dark Morning had ruined that for me. I realized slowly that I had no where to turn. No one to turn too; I could find no comfort. For the first time in my life, I was truly alone. Watching my mother disappear up the path was too much for me to handle. I knew I had to get away.

Not knowing where to go, or what to do with myself; I decided to walk down to the lake. For some reason, I thought I would feel closer to mother if I did so. After walking for a short while I came upon a deserted moss ridden log and decided to sit down. When in the distance I saw Dark Morning approaching. I just continued to sit there, waiting for him.

"Aren't you going to run mud frog? Or maybe you're just too scared?"

I clenched my fists, and looked up into his sadistic gloating face and with squinted eyes I sharply retorted;

"What ever you're going to do, do it and go away. I don't care Anymore! My mothers dead and nothing you can do to me will ever hurt me as much as this. But I want you to know one thing, my mother felt compassion for you. She said you couldn't help being the way you are.

So to honor her memory, I will do as she asked. And no matter what you do to me, I will not hate you for it. So do what you must."

I almost thought my eyes were betraying me, for ever so slowly I saw a gradual change in Dark Morning. At first I was so bent on taking my anger out on this destructive being, that I almost missed it. His once proud shoulders were now slumped downwards in shame. The massive arms that often sought comfort being crisscrossed over his broad chest now hung limply by his side. The continual sneer was now washed away, revealing something I had never seen; someone, alone in the world, just like me.

Shocked and astonished, I couldn't look away. My heart began to relent as remorse coursed through my body in waves. I had no right to vengefully hurt Dark Morning. For I realized that the one thing I had hated the most about him, I had now become. I understood how Dark Morning felt. Like him, I was forced to watch the other families enjoy one another, as we both longed to do.

Remorse soon gave way to compassion as I cleared my throat to speak;

"My mother would not have been proud of me for how I spoke. It is not your fault that she is gone. I will do better the next time we meet."

Breaking his gaze, Dark Morning turned and began shuffling away. I could have been mistaken, but I thought I heard him say; "There won't be a next time."

I continued to sit there, thinking of the astounding transformation I had witnessed. I was grateful for the distraction, as I needed something to take my thoughts off of my mother. And if dissecting the strange behavior of Dark Morning was the best I could do, then so be it.

The next morning I awoke to the sounds of shouting.

"What has he done?! What has he done?!"

Curious by nature, I couldn't help but be enticed by the words being shouted over and over. Quickly I dressed and I stepped out into the open. Hoards of villagers were rushing down towards the lake. Rubbing the sleep from my eyes, I began to follow.

When I had caught up with the others, I slipped through the crowd unnoticed so as to take a peek at what all the shouting was about. The awful spectacle I caught sight of made the air in my chest stop. Sitting in the boggy mud at the lakes edge was Dark Morning's father. He was holding the hand of his only son. Who was dead, laying face down in the mud.

Crying and half shouting, Dark Mornings father started telling all who had gathered what had happened;

"He came and told me what he'd done. I cursed his name and told him that The Great Spirit made a mistake by bringing him into this world. For he had done nothing but cause pain to everyone and everything and I told him that I wish he'd of never been born. That I would have rather had my wife than this horrible twisted boy who stood before me now."

"He said he was throwing stones as far out into the lake as he could, trying to hit the water fowl that his lance had missed.

He said he didn't see her. That he only heard the sound of the water splashing. When he went to investigate, he saw Lake Fishing Woman floating, trapped in her fishing net."

"I asked him why he didn't get someone to help her, and he said the wound on the back of her head was so deep that a piece of the bone was missing. And he knew she was no longer living."

"Not knowing what else to do, he pushed her deeper underwater. Hoping no one would find her."

Gasping for air, Dark Morning's father continued to sob while 2 men from the village picked up his son and carried him away. Feeling a hand on my shoulder was what I needed to tear myself away. It was my father. Unable to look him in the eyes, I asked him if he knew what had happened to Dark Morning. And if it was true what his father had said. My father solemnly nodded and began to speak to me;

"I know you are angrier than you've ever been. But what's done is done. We cannot change what has happened. Dark Morning took his life, in place of your mother's. He consumed the choke berry that grows wild in the forest on the stalky plant. Dark Morning knew he could never repay us while he was alive. So he thought he could repay us with his death."

"Please do not grieve anymore my son. Misfortunes will befall even the wisest of men. Death always comes, and sometimes out of season. But it is the will of The Great Spirit, and we all must obey. What has passed and cannot be prevented must not be grieved over. I know that it seems misfortunes are strong in our lives, but truthfully son, they grow everywhere. Stay strong my son, for our people need you, and I need you."

"Father, what Dark Morning has done confused me. For isn't it the way of our people that if one should accidently take another's life, that the tribal elders and the family of the lost decide what the punishment is?"

"Yes my son. But I think Dark Morning feared he would be judged wrongfully if he was to come forward and admit his wrong doing. You know as well as I do that he has not endeared himself to anyone in the tribe. Unfortunately Dark Morning made his way in life by the teasing and manipulation of others. Which lead to a lifetime of seclusion, ending in a very painful and lonely death."

Quizzically I looked at my father, for sometimes I cannot understand his words. Seeing my puzzled expression, my father continued on with his sentiments;

"Echata, sometimes the best things people have ever done, were done out of remorse for something they had caused. And Dark Morning has fulfilled this. I too grieve the loss of your mother, and I don't know the reason why The Great Spirit called her home. So all I have to offer you are these words I have spoken. As I shall always be like the crippled bird with a broken wing, until my heart is cold within me."

Even though my father offered up his kind words of wisdom, it still left me alone to deal with my pain. Somehow my mother's death seemed worse now, which I didn't think was possible. In three days time, I lost my pet and my mother to a murderous sadistic soul. It seemed that life for me could not get any worse.

From this time on, I had no real memory of passing seasons. I can only remember a sense of great loss as one season blurred into the next, and the next…And the next.

Winters coming was felt once again when it placed its mantle of snow on the surrounding mountain tops. This was the 15th winter since I first drew breath into this world. I remember one evening that early winter I told my father that I felt I was becoming a man. And that I would like to try to live on my own.

"Father, when the snow is gone, I want to build my own lodge down by the lake."

"That's a little far from the heart of the village my son. Are you sure you want to be that far away?"

"I like it down there father. Some how, it makes me feel closer to mother. And when I watch the lake in the evening, I can almost see her walking along the water's edge. When I am quiet and listen to the wind blowing through the lake reeds. It is like she is whispering to me. That place holds many happy memories for me. What I didn't tell my father was that deep inside, I felt cold and disconnected from my people. I felt like none of them wanted me around.

And that they could care less if I lived or died. So why would I want to be their spiritual leader and medicine man?

So the following spring when my father was preparing for another season of work on The Great Stone Circle, I found the perfect spot over looking the lake and I built a small lodge for myself. A stones throw from a stream that fed the 150 acre body of water.

I faced the door of my lodge to the south so that along towards evening when the setting sun cast it's warm golden trails of light down upon the lake, I could sit in my door way and watch the almost hypnotic dance between the light…and the water. All the while reminiscing over the many times I had walked that very lake with my mother.

Living on my own I found was a voluntary seclusion that I enjoyed. My life was lonely, but mostly it existed without the pain and torment that seemed to evolve whenever I was around my people. The peaceful solitude did nothing but increase my bond with my father, for he was always my only visitor.

One day as I walked the edge of the lake with my father, a cry from a bird of prey caught my attention. Quickly I scanned the skies above me seeking the source; There she was, a blindingly beautiful bald eagle riding the currents of brother wind. I stood gazing into the sky with sheer wonderment while she displayed her grace and skill. I said to my father;

"I wish I could have such a beautiful and graceful bird. I would like to snare this creature of the air and tether her leg to a perch outside my lodge. This way I could behold her beauty at my leisure. I really believe this would bring me great joy."

My father replied;

"If you could do such a thing and have this eagle all to yourself, would the eagle still be an eagle?"

"Yes my father. The eagle will always be an eagle no matter where she is. Is this not so?"

"Echata, what makes you love and admire the eagle?"

"That's an easy question." I replied. "For all that the eagle "is" brings me joy of spirit. To watch her soar and be carried aloft on the back of brother wind makes me feel free! With her eyes so keen as to spot a meal so far below and swoop down and capture the animal in such quiet swiftness, I am in awe."

"Is it not so Echata, that if you capture the eagle and tether her to a perch, that you would take away all her attributes that you love and admire? And then will she not be only a shadow of what she once was?"

"Yes my father, thank you for opening my eyes to such a folly. I understand now what you say; For me to take away that which the eagle "is" by her very nature, is to deprive this eagle of her free spirit and making her an eagle no more. So, is there a way that I may get closer to this eagle and not hinder her spirit?"

"Yes my son, there is. Like all things where there is love and respect, there is always a way. Make yourself known to this eagle by making her a food offering.

Do this everyday when the sun is at the same point in the sky and after a time, the eagle will start to trust you. Work with the eagles true nature by coming together on her terms. And one day, she will hunt for you."

The next day, I pondered the insights my father gave me. And I believe this insight is true in all beings. For the things you admire and love cannot be ensnared and confined for you to have for your very own. If you take this away, you end up hurting this love, and their spirit. Leaving them only a shadow of their former self. You must respect that which you love. Allow the freedom, and only by making the offering will you persuade a kinship.

Later in the day and feeling more enlightened than I ever had; I decided to pursue this kinship with the eagle. So with great effort, I followed her to a small valley where I found that she had a nest high on the slope near a rocky outcrop. It took me most of the day to make my way close to her nest where I prepared a food offering for her.

Shortly before sunset, her sharp eyes spied my offering. Her swiftness caught me by surprise! Startling me when she snagged the food offering from my outstretched hand. She circled me once then landed at her nest to eat my offering. I was certain that this first experience with the eagle, is one that will live on in my memory forever. This wonderful happening is the fire that drives me onward.

Each day I made my way up the valley wall close to the rocky outcrop. And each evening she would pluck the food offering from my hand. I found myself feeling more alive than at any other time. Being so close to this raw beauty became intoxicating, and the very thought of her maybe one day landing on my arm exhilarated me!

I truly believed I was forming a bond with sister eagle. For when she saw me sitting near by, she would take to the air and circle. Just waiting for me to extend her food offering in my outstretched hand.

I continued my pursuit of kinship for the rest of the summer. Time and Time again I patiently waited, just hoping she would slow and land on my arm to eat her offering. But alas, my patience was unrewarded. And a great sadness began to set in my heart. This eagle, so beautiful and inspiring was never going to be anything more than something I could admire from a distance. Slowly I realized that what I sought from her was never going to happen.

Needing advice, I summoned my father's wisdom once again.

"My father, again it seems, all that I am left with is sorrow in my heart. My time and effort was wasted on this folly of what might be. Please help me purge this sorrow so that I may feel alive once again."

"My child, you didn't waste your time and effort. Did you not experience this majestic bird closer than at any other time in your life? Did you not say she made you feel alive more than ever? Did she not bring you the hope of possibilities that one day may be?"

"Echata, your adventure with this eagle is a rare and

beautiful thing. Do not spoil your experience because it did not turn out the way you wanted it to. Take from it the good things that you remember, cherishing every moment of pleasure you and the eagle shared."

"Remember, all things in life are like this. Only the possibilities of what may be, is the constant. The rest are all choices one makes along the path."

Knowing that my father was right, I concluded my council by thanking him for opening my eyes, and promising to carry his wisdom for all eternity in my heart.

The next season came and went for me without much notice. And before long, 2 more winters had passed. I had made the decision during this time that I wasn't going to have anything to do with my people. As long as they left me alone, I wasn't going to do anything to change the situation. Until one night…

I had just settled into my lodge and was lying on my back looking at the slits of moonlight that were filtering in through the top of my lodge, thinking to myself; "I'm going to have to fix that before the rains come."

When I noticed something odd, I thought to myself, "What is that sound?…And why do I feel so strange?…Is it the sound of the night birds?…No…The sound of the lake reeds?…That's it!!! .. But it's not the same…It's speaking my name!!!…That can't be!!!"

I held my breath and turned my head from side to side,

trying to locate the direction the sound was coming from. I quickly jumped to my feet and stepped outside and began slowly scanning the outer darkness.

There, in the flickering amber colored light coming from my smoldering fire, stood the image of my mother. She was beckoning to me.

I froze. I fixed my gaze on this beautiful apparition. I couldn't believe what I was looking at. In almost an imperceptible voice I said;

"Mother…Is that you?…"

In a strange and eerie whisper like voice that sounded like the rustling of dry reeds and running water, she said;

"My son, I love you so much…Why are you wasting your life?…You are out here alone and not with your people."

I shook my head as I slowly answered her.

"I just about hate my people…They do nothing but cause me pain…Mother why did you have to go away?…I'm so lonely without you."

I heard the faint sounds of crying coming from my mother as she began to speak to me again.

"My beloved son, I did not go anywhere…I just went out from this earth bound existence. I will always be with you.

And as for our people, you cannot hate them. Or you hate yourself…And me…For we are all apart of each other."

I fell to my knees and began to cry.

"Mother…I could never hate you…"

Her soft and loving voice became so clear to me on the wind as she spoke to me one last time.

"Remember my son…With all your heart…We draw our life from each other…All of us…And you will never be alone."

With this, my mother faded from my sight. I felt a tightening in my chest and throat as a raging torrent of emotion welled up from my inner being. I stood to my feet and looked up to the stars and shouted;
"Mother! I understand. We are all of the same blood. And I will never bring you pain again, for I shall tend to our people!"

The next morning when I awoke, I laid there pondering the events of the previous night. I believe what mother has told me. I shall never be alone. It all seems so clear now. To hate my people is like if I did not like the look of my arm. Should I cut it off and leave it for the wolves? Would I be better for it? I think not. Good or bad, it still serves me.

I knew in my heart at that very moment that I had changed. But I also knew that some of my people would be very hard to deal with. My years of attitude had a way of sticking to me, like mud to my feet after a rain. But I hoped that in time, things would soon change.

At first I didn't know how I was going to "enter" village life, as I had never allowed myself to be a part of it in the past. But The Great Spirit soon made a path for me to follow, when I began to feel an increasing burden for the old ones of the village. I noticed some were not getting enough to eat, and after asking around I learned that they had no living children to take care of them in their old age. This bothered me greatly.

I went and spoke to my father about my findings.

"For one who does not hunt, it must be difficult to carry such a burden. But it might not be so, if one was wise."

Slowly smiling I looked up from the fire I had been poking at with a dry twig.

"Am I in the company of such a person?"

"Some have said so…from time to time."

My father chuckled as he playfully kicked the bottom of my outstretched foot.

"So father, do you see a way for me?"

"Maybe, the other day I was talking with Wee-Sta Noepa (Black-Feather) about his last hunting party. He was telling me of the big bull elk he had taken. When I noticed he needed a new winter coat. You know he doesn't have a wife to make him one. Now, on the other hand we have you. You don't hunt, but you are very skilled in making things. Why not bargain with him? You would both gain. Would you like me to speak with him tomorrow about this?"

I could only smile and nod at my father, for he was so wise. I could always seek his guidance when I was unsure of things.

I had never felt so useful as I did the day I took some dried elk meat to the old ones for them to eat. Maybe it was the sincere smiles and warm hearted "thank you" that propelled me forward on my journey. Maybe I would never know. But for now, this was a new beginning for me. And just as I had found a way to feed the old ones of my village with the help of my father, I felt it gave me a sense of self worth as well.

It wasn't long before I had organized the old ones into a collective bargaining group. I would talk to everyone periodically and take note of the needs and surpluses. And when the time came, I arranged the trades so everyone benefited. I believe this gave the old ones a regained sense of worth as well.

Three more seasons had passed when the day came that my father proudly announced that The Great Stone Circle was completed. Walking up to me and clapping his hand across my back, he proudly announced;

"My son, when spring comes, you are to take your place among your people. You are now the guardian of The Great Stone Circle. And your station in life will now be fulfilled."

I just couldn't believe it! All this time my father and 6 other men left almost every day, and worked from the time the sun came up until the sun passed over the mountains and brought the darkness. All the while I'd never even been allowed to see The Great Stone Circle.

I stammered and stuttered with fearful apprehension;
"Fa..Fa..Father, what am I to do? I still don't have any knowledge of the secret things you told me I would know!"

"Don't worry my son, everything is as it should be. You will know when the time is right. In the coming spring you will go through the purification ceremony. After which you and you alone will enter in the cavern of The Great Stone Circle. Here is where all things will be revealed."

The lingering cold of winter didn't last as long as I had hoped.

Even though my whole life had been spent in preparation of this coming time, the unknown events to come weighed heavily on my mind.

In the early spring my father and I were summoned by the elders. I eagerly rushed to the meeting lodge, not knowing what to expect. There I stood before them with questioning eyes. Wy-Chue-Koe (Ice-Cloud) The oldest member of the council, with wispy low tone in the old mans voice began to speak;

"You are the promised one foretold of by the ancients.

Many lives have been spent preparing the way. Are you ready to do what you must, and take your place as a spiritual leader?"

I responded with a slow nod of my head.

"Go now, and fulfill your destiny, the ancients await!"

Turning, I looked to my father and said;

"Father, I believe it is time to face my death and rebirth into the shaman I am to become. What must I do next?"

"Yet again, you have caused my heart to soar like the mighty hawk upon the wind my son. You are now embracing your life's destiny. We shall begin the purification ceremony on the day of the new coming moon. When we are finished, you will enter cavern of The Great Stone Circle. You will remain there for 3 days. This is the symbolic death and burial of your old way of life."

"During this time, The Great Spirit will give you enlightenment. On the third day you will be reborn as you come from the darkness into the light…my son…once you have done this thing, you will never be the same. You will be much more than you could ever imagine."

We had made the journey back to my fathers lodge by this time, and as we sat down next to the fire, I looked up and stared intently into my fathers eyes for a long while before I began to speak.

"Father…I hope all will be as expected…as of right now, I can't envision such things."

He just chuckled as he firmly griped my shoulder and gave me a reassuring nod.

The days flew by quickly as I patiently waited for the coming new moon. Soon the time was at hand. My father came and took me to a private place he had prepared for the purification ceremony. There he led me through the 7 secret rights of passage, day by day we continued until it was completed.

On the morning of the eighth day we walked to the cavern entrance of Sacred Mountain. On the way there we said very little to each other.

When we reached the entrance, my father only said this;

"Burn only one torch at a time, that way you will have enough for the three days you're in there."

He backed away from me raising his hands. And with tears in his eyes he looked up to the heavens and loudly proclaimed;
"I give my son, Echata-Quai-Atoke to mother earth. And in three days, The Great Spirit shall give him back to me!!"

With this said, he turned and started back towards the village. I watched him until he disappeared from my sight. I said to myself; "father never looked back or slowed his step, I must do the same." With a deep breath, I turned and made my way several feet down inside the tunnel. Here I came upon the pile of torches my father had told me about. I took out one of my flints and picked up a torch to light. After setting the torch ablaze, I then continued my descent into the cavern.

After what seemed to be several hundred paces, the cavern passage began to open up. I stopped for a moment and squinted my eyes, I stared intently into the blackness hoping to be able to see something. Reaching out, I could only feel the cold smooth dampness of the solid stone that surrounded me. A wave of gut tightening anguish passed over me as I thought to myself;

"This is much like the cave of whispering souls…I must not think of such things."

I started remembering a song my mother taught me as a child, I began singing it as I continued along my way. This distraction brought me great comfort as I recited the words and thought of my mother.

It was the song of round things, I sang to myself; "How many things are round?…The sun…the moon…my eyes…a basket…my lodge." About the third time through the song, I finally entered the main cavern chamber.

I stopped abruptly and gasped out loud. There in the middle of the huge open cavern was The Great Stone Circle. In the pale amber light of the flickering torch, I could just make out the sheer size of it.

"it must be ten full paces across the middle!"

I slowly walked around the outside of The Great Stone

Circle to study my surroundings. I noticed a row of twenty four evenly spaced torches around the perimeter of the cavern. I lit the first torch nearest the opening I had came through. This added more light and made it easier for me to see everything. I squatted and fixed my gaze up on The Great Stone Circle and felt a little disappointed, yet relieved.

It just didn't look as ominous as I thought it was going to. I quickly lost my fearful apprehension. Knowing it was going to be a long wait, I slowly backed up and sat down next to the wall.

Time for me is not measured in minutes or by hours. I have no concept of the mechanical measurement of passing moments. There are only things I know in nature, such as the path of the sun across the sky and the cycles of the moon. Slow change of seasons is noticed by the winters cold snows to the late summers heat accompanied by the coming and going of migratory animals.

So, for me, in the heart of this mountain and not being able to see anything for a point of reference, it became sheer agony not knowing how long I'd been in this place. The only thing that kept me from losing my mind, was what my father had told me.

"That on the morning of the third day, the watchers will come for you, they will wait at the entrance and beat the drum."

Not knowing what to do, I just waited…I slept from time to time, and as I lit each torch and it slowly burned away, I would wonder to myself, "how long have I been in here? Will I be enlightened before the next torch burns away?"

When I was down to my last five torches, I began to panic. For I had been in this cave for 2 and a half days and nothing had happened, I still didn't feel any closer to The Great Spirit than when I first arrived! And I certainly didn't feel any more enlightened.

I walked over and stood in front of The Great Stone Circle. With my youthful pride and cockiness now drained from me, I fell to my knees and cried out to The Great Spirit;

"What must I do?…What am I to tell my people?…I cannot face them with nothing to tell them!"

Now for the first time since I had entered the cavern, I was truly broken in spirit and humbled. I began to agonize over my situation when a strange feeling began to overcome me. My mind began to clear and fill with a wonderful song. I was quickly strengthened and words came to me of what to say and do.

I jumped to my feet and began to chant;

"Of mother earth and father sky…from mighty sun to sister moon…from the East, South, West, and North…I call upon brother wind…gentle as the summer breeze…and strong as the winter storms…breathe upon me insight of The Great Spirit…for I am they that walked before me…I am the same as a drop of rain, or the majestic mountain…for once what was…shall be again!!!"

I reached out and took hold of the obelisks at the front of The Great Stone Circle. In that instance I felt part of my life force go out of me and enter into The Great Stone Circle. The ground trembled and I heard the mountain groan. I then heard what sounded like many whispering voices as I was surrounded by rushing wind. I felt energized!

With each beat of my heart a very faint blue light began to emanate from within the center of the circle. With each beat, it grew brighter and brighter until the entire cavern was aglow with the pale blue light.

My mind began to fill with wondrous sights and sounds that blended in with my own thoughts. It was as if I had lived the lives of each of the 12 generations of builders. I was experiencing all of their love, learning and trials of life. Then suddenly, I understood it all!! Some how, some way as each of the builders went about their building tasks, The Great Stone Circle absorbed all of their life experiences. Now, I had the accumulated knowledge of all of the builders from beginning to end.

I knew why and how it was built. Its function and purpose became clear. It was not only a storage device and a link to my ancestors, it was an enablement for the vision quest. Many times in my life I'd heard of tribal elders, including my father, speak of a vision quest. When ever I would question them about it, they explained it to me this way;

In a vision quest, a person enters a spiritual dream like state. While in this state, he can communicate with the spirit guides or his ancestors. This helps the seeker to work through his problems and serves to make him stronger.

When my mind finally cleared, I became aware that I was no longer standing and holding on to the obelisks of The Great Stone Circle. I felt the cold hard cavern floor pushing up against my back. Slowly I opened my eyes and gazed at the cavern ceiling, which was being bathed in the soft pale blue light.

Sitting up, I looked with sheer wonderment upon this amazing circle of light. In my mind, I could still feel a connectedness to the builder's memories. I arose and walked over to examine the alternating blocks of stone that made up the structure.

This one that glows with the blue light is the rare clear water stone that has bits of sunlight trapped in it…how can a stone look like ice, and yet not melt?…these were the ones that were hardest to work with…we could not do it ourselves… The Great Spirit told us where to find the heavy black rock that bleeds when it gets wet. We took it and crushed it into powder. Then we poured it into lines on the clear water stone where we wanted to break it. We then took dried hollow reeds from the lake and filled them with the powdered black rock, and lashed them onto long poles. We would then place these poles on the powdered rock lines and raise the other end to the sky.

We would then leave and wait for the storm clouds to come. The Great Spirit would send the light from the sky that touched the poles. And with more noise than a great falling tree, the clear water stone would then be broken along the black powdered rock lines.

The next stone, in between the clear water stones, is cousin to the heavy black rock that bleeds. Only these ones pull toward one another and will stick to each other. They were easier to break. We would take a shard of the clear water stone and place it in the end of a straight stick, and slowly rotate the shard end on a cut line and this would slowly bore a hole into the rock. This would be done all along the break lines. After this, dry wooden sticks would be driven into the holes and we would wait for the rains to come. Then after 2 or 3 days, the stone would be broken in two.

The Great Stone Circle is made in the following manner; there are 12 black stones that are the width and height of a man's arm, and 2 arms in length. Then there are 13 clear water stones of the same size. Except 2 of the clear water stones have a square cut obelisk the length of an arm mounted on one end.

The circle starts with an obelisk bearing block followed by a black stone block, each one fitted tight against the another, alternating all the way around the circle and finally ending with an obelisk bearing block.

But these two do not touch, as there is a gap the width of a mans hand between the two obelisk bearing blocks, and when I placed my hands on the obelisks, I became the link that completes the circle.

I slowly began pondering the coming year. I realized that

with this new access to the great wealth of knowledge I had just encountered, that I would be able to formulate a good plan of guidance for the upcoming year.

I was so engrossed in my thinking that finally, after several minutes, I began to become aware of the sound of a faint drum echoing down the passageway. I realized that it was time to go and be reborn into the light of day. And with that, I pulled a lit torch from the wall and started back up the passageway.

When I reached the opening of the cavern, just as he had promised, my father was there waiting for me. I could tell by his expression that the 3 days I was inside, was almost more than he could tolerate. Upon seeing me emerge from the cavern, his first words were rushed.

"My son, what is to become of our people?"

"Father, our people shall have no worries any longer. For I have been enlightened in a way that shall enable me to seek guidance for us whenever is needed. We are no longer strangers in this land."

During Echata's lifetime, he called upon The Great Stone Circle many times. He also sought the vision quest every year in the spring, so as to have proper direction to guide his people.

Echata was so conscious of his people's needs, that he never took a wife. He felt He was enough of a burden to his people, for they supplied all his needs. Like new moccasins as needed and deerskin pants and shirt once a year, as well as warm elk skin robes for the winter. He never even worried about his meals for he always had lots of invitations. But a man who does not hunt, to take a wife would be shameful. A man who does not supply his family's needs is no good. So Echata felt that he was just not in the position to take a wife.

This meant that Echata would have to select a child from someone else to train as his apprentice. He was saddened knowing that his bloodline ended with him. And this fact always bothered him and caused him to procrastinate. And when it came to selecting such a child, he would say to himself; "When I am getting on in years I will find someone." Unfortunately, time has a way of slipping away.

34 winters had now passed since Echata came into this world. And in the early summer of that year, Echata was called to the lodge of an old woman named Tona-Acha Kimtai (Shining Red Earth) he tended to the old one and found that she was feverish. He pulled some dried herbs from his medicine sack and said;

"Put this in some water and drink it. It should help you for now, but I will have to go south of here a days walk where the grove of alder trees are. In the clearing that is near by is where the Joia root grows. It must be soaked in water with the bark of the Whaina Wheesh. you will then drink this water, and it will take away the heat in your face and make you well. I will be back in 2 days to make the medicine."

The next morning at first light, Echata gathered his digging tools and medicine bag. He set out across the village towards the south. The travel was easy going this time of year as it was dry and warm.

By late afternoon, he arrived at the alder grove. Wasting no time, Echata pulled his digging tools from his medicine bag. Quickly he stepped out into the clearing and began scanning the ground for the small white flower of the Joia plant. Before long he had found a nice big one. He knelt down and began digging in the dry hard earth. He mumbled to himself;

"Thirsty earth is always slow digging"

Suddenly, Echata felt his body slam to ground and his breath rush out of him. A loud ringing filled his ears as his body began hitting the ground again and again. Then everything became very still. He slowly opened his eyes…He realized he had been reliving his life's memories. The weakness in his body was overwhelming. Summoning the last of his strength, he said;

"With my last breath, I shall give my spirit to the wind…I must go and make search of someone to tell of my life… Of mother earth and father sky…from mighty sun to sister moon…From the East, South, West and North…I call upon brother wind…Gentleness of the summer breeze…And Strength of the winter storms…Come catch my spirit brother wind! Lift me high upon the breath of The Great Spirit…For I am they that walked before me…I am the same as a drop of rain or the majestic mountain…For what once was…Shall be again…

PART 2
A new soul is born.

After the death of the medicine man, Joy Of The Soaring Hawk. The guidance and social structure of the Stone Circle Tribe (No-Cha Quaia Ma-Ko) fragmented. The many years of uncertainty took its toll, causing the population to slowly dwindle.

It is the nature of The Great Spirit the nothing is ever left undone. And in the fullness of time, The Great Spirit will always provide a way.

Many generations passed before an enlightened soul felt the burden for the people. This soul was a boy child born to Elk woman (Saws-Na Oo-Ma-Hai-o) and Blue Hand (Pai-Qua Chen-Ah). In the manor long in practice by The Stone Circle Tribe, a child is always called by their parents name. This remained so unless they had earned a name the tribe would call them openly.

One hot august afternoon, when the son of Blue Hand was about nine winters old, he said to his father;

"I have noticed the old ones of the village, they are not doing so well. Some are sick from lack of meat. Why is this happening father?"

"It has been a long hot summer with very little rain, and when this happens, the deer and elk go high to the coolness of the mountain slopes. They will not come back down until the snows come and drive them out."

"Is there anything we can do for the old ones? For I have seen the look of hunger in their faces father."

"I wish there were. We are running low on dried meats, and if we aren't blessed by the cool of the coming winter, we will all be going hungry."

Blue hand slowly squatted, reaching down he clutched a hand full of parched earth. With a deep sigh he said;

"If only we had not lost touch with The Great Spirit."

With a puzzled look of concern the boy said;

"How did that happen father?"

Blue hand frowned and shook his head as he began to speak;

"After Joy of The Soaring Hawk was killed, our ancestors became frightened.

They thought The Great Spirit was angry with us. So the tribal elders felt it best not to call upon The Great Spirit. And as the years passed, no one was willing to take a chance with trying to seek guidance from The Great Spirit. This is why our tribe is no longer known as The Children Of The Great Spirit.

(Chono-Oo-Ee Pay B-Doda). We call ourselves the Stone Circle People. (No-Cha Quaia—Ma—ko). This reminds us of what we have lost. Our link to our ancestors and the guidance of The Great Spirit. Maybe someday The Great Spirit will look upon us with pity and grant us his favor."

Later that day, the boy came to his father and asked;

"Father, do you think the elders would become angry if I sought The Great Spirit in behalf of our tribe & ask his forgiveness?"

"No, they don't believe in much of anything anymore son."

"Well I am going to the central meeting place in our village. There I will dance before The Great Spirit and sing of his mighty nature. Then I will ask his blessing upon our tribe."

Blue hand chuckled to himself as he mused over the innocence of youth.

As evening drew near, Blue Hand could still hear his son in the distance singing and pounding a drum. He thought to himself, "I Better go get him and bring him back to the lodge before someone becomes annoyed with him."

Upon coming in close view of his son, Blue Hand was shocked by his son's appearance. There he was, dancing up a cloud of dust as he croaked out his song of praise to The Great Spirit. He looked very tired and in pain. Blue Hand motioned for his son to stop and said;

"Maybe it is time for you to come back to the lodge with me."

His boy stumbled over to where he was standing and looked up at him and in a trembling voice said;

"Father! I cannot! Please don't make me stop!"

Blue Hand looked at the dust covered face of his son, seeing the tears welling in his eyes Blue Hand's spirit began to sore as he was filled with pride. He now realized that his son's heart was pure and full of selfless motivation. His moment of joy was quickly replaced by pangs of shame. Realizing his son was doing what the whole tribe should have been doing long ago.

Blue Hand said;

"If you can't stop, then I shall help you sing!"

With that being said, he took his boy's drum and began to play and chant for his son. It wasn't long before the tribal elders had gathered around to see what was going on. Seeing Blue Hand and his son and hearing their songs, the spirits of the tribal elders were lifted and they joined in as well and sang late into the night.

The next day, Blue Hand and his son were summoned before the elders.

The spokesman for the elders said;

"From this day forth, the son of Blue Hand will be called "Spirit Singer". (Whai-Yatai Nako). And when his name is spoken, it will remind us of his selfless act. It took a brave heart for this young boy to act in behalf of his tribe. His efforts to reunite his people with The Great Spirit have been heard. No one has ever done such a thing since the great medicine man Joy of The Soaring Hawk."

Spirit Singer realized at that moment, that his path was not going to be the way of the warrior, but the way of the Shaman medicine man.

***

As the years passed Spirit Singer found that learning the ways of the medicine man came easily to him. One particular area he excelled at was communing with the spirit world. He easily reached through the vale that separated their 2 realms. His newly found talent showed him the way to become a healer, councilor and dream interpreter.

Spirit Singers name suited his qualities well. For his uniqueness in interpreting dreams was a medicine all his own. The tribes people believing that the interpretation of dreams was necessary due to that most dreams were plainly indicative of the future.

Along with many fine qualities Spirit Singer possessed, none was greater to him than his medicine bundle. Made with great care from the pelt of a silver fox, Spirit Singer placed several items inside of symbolic value to him.

Included inside was his medicine pipe, 4 arrow heads, dried tobacco, sage and red cedar shavings.

Spirit Singers days were long. For he took it upon himself to try and walk in the disintegrated footsteps of the once great medicine man, Joy Of The Soaring Hawk. He soon found this path was not simple. It required much knowledge that he didn't have. And consequently he spent all his time in the pursuit of his new position as medicine man, which left little time for anything else.

Being appointed the tribes Holy man was the most significant thing that had happened to Spirit Singer. With this title came duty, honor, respect and responsibility. To insure his success, He was to attend the yearly gathering of medicine men. This even took place in the early spring. The yearly medicine men gathering consisted of 3 long days of talks with all the neighboring tribes.

Beings Spirit Dreamer was appointed the tribes Holy man during the Winter meant he had to wait until spring to attend his first meeting. Waiting for the snow to melt was very agonizing.

One early morning, while Spirit Singer was checking on the needs of the village, he came upon the lodge of Black Crow. (Awake-Na) As he stepped inside the round earthen structure and stamped the snow from his feet, his eyes were immediately drawn to the beautiful woman sitting by the fire. Startled back to attention by the gentle clearing of Black Crow's throat, Spirit Singer quickly accepted the warm, dried meat that was offered to him. Focusing on the task at hand,

Spirit Singer asked Black Crow if there was anything that his family was in need of.

Fighting his urge to ignore Black Crow, Spirit Singer listened intently as he told him what they were in need of. After making note, he realized that the beautiful woman he saw by the fire was in fact Black Crow's daughter. His mind wandered back to the summer when he heard the women in the fields hoeing and singing to the corn. Among them was now more beautiful than ever, Awake-Na Gapoe (Black Crow's Daughter) This was the first time he could ever remember seeing her. But surely she wasn't this beautiful then…or was she?

Impulsively he asked Black Crow if he would allow his daughter to go with him to finish his tasks. Without waiting for her father to answer for her, Black Crow's Daughter swept past her father and landed beside Spirit Singer and said to him;

"Where are we going today?"

Looking to her father for his approval of the venture, Spirit Singer was relieved when Black Crow slowly nodded his head in acceptance. For if you were to take a Daughter from her family without their consent, you would suffer considerable shame. And this would not be looked upon lightly. The same goes for thief or the liar. You will branded and such for your lifetime. And shame was not a brand he wished to have placed upon him.

Leaving their lodge, Black Crow's Daughter just couldn't believe how much she had been blessed by The Great Spirit!

She had always admired Spirit Singer but he never seemed to notice her until today. She wondered to herself; "What has changed? Have I grown taller? Has my hair grown longer?" Whatever it was, she didn't care, for at this moment she could only focus on the man beside her.

They walked in silence for a few minutes as Spirit Singer couldn't think of anything to say. He didn't even know why he had felt the urge to ask for her to come with him. Finally breaking the silence, Black Crow's Daughter spoke first.

"I don't know why you asked me to come along, but whatever the reason, I am thankful for your kindness."

Still not able to recover from his impulsiveness, he could only manage to smile and Nod in her direction. For the sound of her soft voice only further unnerved him. He chose to concentrate on the sound his moccasins made as they crunched through the ice covered snow.

As they walked in silence with only the sound of the snow between them, Spirit Singer began to feel more and more at ease with his traveling companion.

Soon, without thinking, he began to speak his mind;

"I think this winter is the coldest I can ever remember. My friend One Rattle Shaking (O-Whap-O Whapee-Tai) told me that his father had only seen the lake freeze over 1 other time."

Shocked by his sudden change, Black Crow's Daughter

was more than ready to respond to just about anything Spirit Singer could say;

"I know what you mean. My father said we would have to be careful with our dried meats, as winter is going to last longer than usual."

"Yes, the deer and elk stay farther south when the winters are long."

They continued walking in silence for a short while longer, when Spirit Singer blurted out;

"I want to take you for my wife."

Stammering Black Crow's Daughter said;
"What???!!!"

"You heard me, I want to take you for my wife."

"But you hardly know me!"

"You say I hardly know you, but what else do I need to know? Other than as I look upon you this morning, I realize love is something we must share between us. We need it as our spirit chief needs our praise. We must have it or our self esteem will become weak and faint. Without it our courage will fail and we will no longer be able to look out on to the world with confidence. I heard of your coming when I was many steps away. And I never made such attempts before. I knew you were to do good for me, and I for you. And just as this shallow brook swells with water from the melting snow, my heart fills with joy when I gaze upon you."

"I seek the comfort, the undeniable comfort of feeling safe when you are with a person. I do not have to weigh my thoughts or measure my words. They pour out of my heart and through my mouth all of them right to you, just as they are. Rough and strewn together, I am certain your faithful hand will take and sift through them and keep what is worth keeping. And with your heavenly breath of love, blow the rest away."

"Do you still say I do not know you? Well my dove, it is true I know I love you only. Your heart is as sweet as the juice that drips from your lips as you pluck my heart from my chest with your smile. My spirit says I need you and that is good enough for me."

Black Crow's Daughter stopped walking and put her hand on Spirit Singers' arm. Upon seeing the look in her beautiful black eyes, he knew her words need not be spoken. Turning towards her, he gently reached out his hand and tipped her face towards his;

"Upon our return, I shall tell your father that I love his daughter. I will ask him to give you to me so that the roots of my heart may entangle with yours, so in case the strongest wind of life may blow, we shall never part."

Walking back to the lodge, Black Crow's Daughter gently slipped her fur trimmed hand into his and at that moment, Spirit Singer knew he had made the right decision. The Great

Spirit opened his eyes to see this truly marvelous creature that walked beside him now. And for that he was entirely thankful.

Winter's cold didn't seem to last long, as before Spirit Singer knew, it was time for the annual meeting of the medicine men. This was a very exciting time for him, as this would be his first meeting. He said to his new wife;

"I've heard this meeting is very important and all must attend! Something is happening that may change our way of life."

"Well then you should go with much haste my husband, our life seems to be dependent upon this."

After collecting the things for his trip, he hastily gave parting words to his wife and set out for the gathering.

When Spirit Singer arrived at the meeting, he met up with 2 of his longtime friends, Sky Blue Face (Hai Chen-Ahh) & One Rattle Shaking (O—Whap-O Whapee-Tai.) He asked his friends;

"Have you heard anything about the gathering?"

Sky Blue face responded;

"Word is that it's about the coming of the white man. They have been seen as close as ten days walk from here! Some of the other tribes want to form war parties drive them away."

Spirit Singer said;
"I don't blame them. I hear they are sickly creatures with bad tempers."

One Rattle Shaking added;

"They are a heartless and cruel beast that attack tribes for no reason!

The three men gathered close and spoke of fearful things that may come, long into the night. The next day, word was sent for all to gather in the great lodge. This heavy round structure was built around a wide depression in the ground. In the center is a rock fire pit. Here is where a person would take up issues with the elder medicine men who sat in the outer circle

***

Pushing their way in through the lodge doorway, the men commented to each other how crowded it was. People were rubbing against them on all sides. Standing in the blackness and waiting for his eyes to adjust, the smell of cedar smoke hung thick in the air. The blackness slowly gave way to dim flickers of amber colored firelight. Spirit Singer heard a familiar voice in the distance, someone was already making a fiery speech before the council of medicine men.

It was the Sly One. (Cayuse Ka) He was the medicine man of the Paiute tribe from the south. His pompous and intolerant reputation preceded him. There he was in all his glory, parading back and forth showing off his feathered attire like some strutting rooster. As he spoke, at times he would break into screaming like a madman. He was saying;

"I know we have all heard the rumors of the white man. And some of us have seen one or two that live in the mountains and hunt the fur of the animals. Or the strange ones that dig in the earth in search of the yellow metal. But I tell you this; I have been far to the southwest with one I know from the Seattle tribe. He took me to a place where I could see a white mans village."

"These creatures are very strange. They cut down the trees and build their lodges In the open where they have no wind break to guard against the drifting snows of the winter. Their lodges are built with four flat sides and placed in rows next to one another."

"They have no sense of family and are strangers to one another. They are violent and kill each other over arguments. These dim witted hairy faced killers lay in wait for any opportunity to prey on the weak!"

"But this is not the worst of it! I will make tell of what I have heard."

"Many seasons walk in the direction of the rising sun is where they come from.

And in that place are others of our kind. This white man has killed more of our kind than can be counted. Whole nations have been driven away! They do not even spare women or children. Their blood lust is never satisfied!"

"That is only part of their curse! For they also carry sickness and spread it to all they touch! I was told of a time when a tribe came across two starving white travelers. They took pity on them and took them in. And it wasn't long before the whole tribe was stricken with sickness and all of them died! Surely these creatures must be evil outcasts from The Great Spirit. For they war against his nature and give nothing back to mother earth."

"We must unite in a great war party and drive this intruder out! We must never let them build a lodge in our area. If we do, more of them will come, and in the end, we will all suffer the untold anguish from this miserable creature!"

A man in the outer circle shouted out;

"I have seen a dead one up close, his hair was the color of smoldering fire and his eyes the color of the sky."

This was bad timing on his part with all the previous talk of sickness. Several of the men standing around this fellow became panic stricken. They started pushing away from him and shouting;

"If you touched him, then get away from me!"

This kind of thing is what The Sly One is known for, stirring up the people.

He knew he had sewn the seeds of panic, but now he must

control what he had started. The Sly One called out to the man in the outer circle;

"Calm yourselves! How long has it been since you seen the dead man?"

He replied;

"About five moons ago."

The Sly One said;
"It will be all right, the sickness they carry acts very quickly. They have heat in their face and round marks on their body the color of blood. If he had it, you would have died within one moon's passing."

The uneasiness that filled the crowd of men gave the Sly One a thrilling sense of accomplishment. For he knew he needed the majority of supporters in order to be granted war party status.

The spokesman for the elder medicine men stood up and said;
"We will speak of this more tomorrow, after we have considered this matter further. You are all excused for the day."

Later that evening, several small groups of men, including Spirit Singer, Sky Blue Face and one Rattle shaking had gathered around the central meeting area on their own accord. They were discussing with growing concern what had happened at the meeting.

Spirit Singer and his two friends were squatting next to a cooking fire, when One Rattle Shaking said;

"The old Sly One's words burn in my stomach. They make my heart fear. I don't like this feeling. It reminds me of what my Father told me about him."

Spirit Singer said;

"I feel the same, but we all know how the Sly One is. One never knows how much is truth and how much is for show. So much killing is hard to grasp. Brother, what is it that you know?"

Pondering what Spirit Singer said, One Rattle Shaking decided to tell the others what he'd learned about "The Old Sly One". Shifting uneasily and inching forward to get closer to the fire, One Rattle Shaking cleared his voice and began his story;

"Our tribal history says that two brave and skillful young hunters, members of the Paiute Tribe; ventured far beyond the realm of the living. They went where the ancients told dwelt The Great Spirit. A land of spirits reached only by way of a mighty cavern, which led into the regions of the unholy. Here they were taught that all unworthy men returned to dwell."

"They described it as a place as deep and endless as the very sky. Where Mountains sank into the bottomless depths of the spiritual world. A domed peak they said arose from near the center of this unbounded depth. This was the throne of the unholy himself. Within this dome was a white hot fire that billowed forth blue flames and graying smoke. Struggling about the smoking cloud that encircled the mouth of this crater where winged spirits, attempting to escape their firey prison. But they were bound by the will of The Great Spirit. These were the remnants of evil men that are doomed to suffer an eternal penalty of torture for all their earthy wrong doings."

"In the bottom of this massive abyss of torture was a sheet of water as blue as the sky in which it reflected. Over the surface and on the surrounding banks dwelled the spirits of the departed. They sailed the glossy depths in gilded canoes, while others roamed the tranquil shades of the forest in search of game."

Breaking the silence of One Rattle Shaking's brief pause was the sound of footsteps treading lightly all around them. The three men turned to see that a small crowd had gathered to listen to One Rattle's eloquent and mystical tale.

Clearing his throat so as to speak a little louder, he continued the recount of his story;
"They often flew like flocks of birds from one pinnacle to another. Some even dared to fish the crystal waters. Here on earth the paradise, and in the crater stood the unholy."

"The warriors were warned that only the medicine men were allowed by The Great Spirit to visit this seemingly uholy retreat. For as this was where they came and counseled with him; even meeting with the dead ones of the tribe and bore messages from them to the living. Here they would gather medicine for the sick and produce charms for the fate of the living."

"These medicine men declared that it was the decree of The Great Spirit that if any living man who should dare to intrude upon the sacred presence of the dead, should also die in consequence and be cast out and cursed to reside inside the firey dome."

"The warriors felt they were brave and feared not even The Great Spirit. For both wore the scalps of other many mighty warriors at their belts. They had fought and battled the fiercest beats of the forest; they'd overcome all enemies they had ever chanced to meet. Becoming bored, they longed for fresh adventures with thrilling dangers that rivaled each other's courage."

"Hearing of others being able to pass through the veils into the realm of the unholy, was the challenge both the warriors sought. They wasted no time in entering the forest, traveling east towards the sky towering pinnacles. On they pressed, dauntless in their courage until they reached the regions of the unholy.

They climbed higher and nearer towards the great abyss. At last they came upon a break in the forest. It was as it had been described to them. In awe of its power and mightiness, both the warriors were transfixed to their spots."

"There, as the ancient medicine man had foretold; lay the bluest lake they had ever seen. Their eyes caught sight of odd spirits with wings like birds. And in the middle of the placid water stood a mountainous dome that spewed forth flames and smoke; intermingled with the agonizing cries of suffering men.

The screams of the tortured comingled with the screeches of the bird like spirits."

"The warriors stood and gazed, unable to tear themselves away until at last The Great Spirit; ever conscious of the movements of all man, summoned the huge monster from within the depths of the lake and pointed to the two men standing at the edge of the realm. The great dragon like beast wanting to do the bidding of his master, sliced through the tranquil surface of the lake with its hundred fins; and with a giant leap, the water dragon cleared the high precipice and ensnared one of the warriors with his enormous clawed foot and dragged him back down into the darkest depths."

"The other warrior, The Old Sly One; fled instantly at the approach of the dragon and ran wildly back down the mountain. Myriads of spirits now disturbed by the thunderous boom of the dragon, and with more speed than a lightening arrow, they ignited into flight chasing after the lone warrior."

"He ran harder and faster than he had ever run. Stumbling through the underbrush and cutting his legs as he leaped over fallen trees and moss covered boulders. The spirits, relentless in their pursuit; swooped down and began targeting his limbs for removal. He dashed on safely reaching his tribes settlements. He proclaimed loudly for all to hear, the fate of his doomed companion."

"The eldest member of the tribe called forth his treacherous actions as a tremendous offense against The Great Spirit. He warned The Old Sly One that he must fulfill the stern decree of The Great Spirit. That he now must yield his soul in death, to undergo the tortures that are now awaiting him in the firey dome."

"Upon hearing his true fate, The Old Sly One begged and pleaded with the elders. He was convinced that he could somehow repay his treacherous offense.

The Old Sly One then proclaimed that he would take on the burdens of the tribe and try to repay his debt."

"As time went on, it was said that he became bitter and cold. And has no love left inside him for any of his kind. He considers us all a foe. And as of late, it seems he spends most of his time trading with these gray eyed hairy faced settlers."

Upon completion, One Rattle Shaking was startled to learn that his tale had drawn the attention of the oldest shaman known to exist, "Tut-Tu Naw-Saw (Many Storms) Quickly, One Rattle Shaking bowed his head and dropped down on his right knee and stamped his medicine staff 3 times on the ground;
Thus paying respect to the old one.

Many Storms' voice was raspy and hollow when he told One Rattle Shaking that his "respect was noted". As One Rattle Shaking resumed his position next to his 2 friends, the old man crept through the now parting crowd to rest his battered and weathered body against a pole.

To be in the presence of such a highly powerful shaman was a very rare thing. So the utmost respect is to be given at all times. No one is to speak unless the old man grants you permission. Silence is meaningful, and the granting of a space of silence before one talks is the practice of extreme politeness. And always mindful of the rule that "Thought comes before the speech." None of the men knew why they had drawn the attention of the old one.

But luckily enough, the old man wasted no time in getting to the reason he had joined the men;

"I hear you speak of The Sly One's fate. For I know the story well. But I ask you men this, do you know of the lake in which this happened? We elders have been seeking guidance from The Great Spirit since The Sly One's journey.

We are in fear that if he does not submit to the decree of The Great Spirit, that it will anger him and he will call forth the spirits in the mountains to bring destruction upon our people."

"I feel I must make tell of another time when we were not living harmoniously; when our people suffered in sadness and destruction as the spirits raged around us in a mighty war that destroyed our lands."

"As you all may know, the mountain to our east, "Lee-Whal Alta" (The One Whom Smokes Comes), her forests are never hunted, nor is her lake ever fished.

We give great respect so as not to anger her. She was once a cherished, wrinkled old woman who went by the name of "Loo-Whit-Ka Loo". (Lady of Fire) She lived on a great land bridge that stretched across the mighty river. Her job was simple, but important to us all. Loo-Whit-Ka Loo tended the sacred flame that The Great Spirit sent to us from the sky. Every few days, a fire warrior would be sent from the tribes on each side of the river. She would then give them a torch set aflame from her sacred fire which they would then take back to their village to rekindle the smoldering ashes."

"Loo-Whit-Ka Loo's faithfulness in her task was so extraordinary that she was noticed by The Great Spirit. So to reward her for her kindness, The Great Spirit decided to bestow a gift upon Loo-Whit-Ka Loo. One that was only given to a seldom few; The gift of eternal life. Though she graciously accepted her gift, she began to weep openly while thanking The Great Spirit. Confused by her tears of pain, The Great Spirit asked Loo-Whit-Ka Loo what was wrong. She responded in kind by saying; "I thank you Great Spirit, but I do not wish to live forever in the body of a grizzled old woman." Not wanting to disappoint her again, The Great Spirit let her know that he could not take back the gift he'd given. So to ease her suffering, he granted her one wish."

"Loo-Whit-Ka Loo quickly answered by asking to once again be the beautiful young maiden she was in her youth. The Great Spirit granted her wish and before long, the fame of her wondrous beauty coupled with her empathy for all life, spread far and wide across the land like a wild fire pushed by the hot summer wind."

"The stories of the beautiful maiden eventually reached the ears of 2 powerful spirits by the name of Llao and Skell. These 2 bothers were sentenced to an eternal life of separation and servitude by The Great Spirit. Llao was master of every living thing under the earth and water. And his brother Skell, was the master of all living animals above the earth."

"Llao, being the most evil of the 2, was sentenced to live out eternity in the firey domed peak in which you spoke of earlier. He spent his days and nights serving the most evil and wicked of spirits. Skell, having the lessor penalty, was allowed to live among the very creatures he once tortured and killed. Eternally serving these animals was his prison."

"In time, the 2 once loving brothers slowly became ferocious mortal enemies due to the love they both shared for Loo-Whit-Ka Loo. The blood lust Llao developed for Skell couldn't be stopped. It was truly the nature of the beast.

He was miserable being immersed in a sea of fire and cruelty and welcomed his perverse nature to change his immortal body. His gnarled fingers and jagged nails raked through his patchy black hair as he paced his dungeon watching from below while his peaceful brother roamed the tree lined shores above with Loo—Whit-Ka Loo."

"Finally having had enough, Llao commanded his brother Skell to deliver Loo-Whit-Ka Loo to him in 3 days, or else 7 days of death and destruction would be launched upon the very tribes Loo-Whit-Ka Loo helped. Fearless of his brothers threats, Skell began moving the tribes far away from Llao's lair. Seeing Skell help the natives enraged him so much, that Llao rose up from inside the domed peak and hurtled a white hot boulder at Skell, momentarily penning him to the ground so that Llao's winged spirits could carve his brother's beating heart from his body and deliver back to him."

"Stricken by grief, Loo-Whit-Ka Loo gathered with the animals and bewailed their fate of their master. Just then, a messenger appeared to them, proclaiming Llao to be the master of all living things above the earth, as well as all things below. After the spirit messenger left, a coyote said to Loo-Whit-Ka Loo;"

"Since it is known that Skell will live again if his heart is returned to his body, let us proceed to Llao's home and declare ourselves his loyal subjects so we may await the moment when we can return our masters heart to his body."

"Taunts greeted them when they arrived in the land of Llao. One ruthless follower grabbed the heart of Skell and began tossing it in the air. The coyote annoyed by this action, began to chide the ruthless one for not being able to toss it very far. Other followers began to join in and try to toss it too, but the coyote still chided them all for not being able to throw it high enough into the air. Finally, Llao became angry at his taunts and stalked out and hurled it high into the air. It soared and soared and finally came to the ground at the edge of the forest."

"The fox who was hidden near by in the brush, snatched it and rushed into the forest. All of Llao's followers began to chase the fox, and just as they were about to catch him, an antelope burst through the group and took the heart and rushed on with it. Then the mighty eagle swooped in, and taking the heart from the antelope, flew out of sight with it. Within moments, a voice of a dove sounding from a great distance, announced that Skell lived again."

"Llao, brooding over his loss of triumph, sought out Skell in his own land and challenged him to a wrestling match. Skell knew that Llao was stronger, but decided to wrestle instead of looking cowardly before his love. Llao quickly grabbed Skell and threw him over his shoulder and started towards his home.

When they were only a short distance away, Skell said a louse was biting him and needed to scratch. Llao taunted him by saying; "What matter a little bite when I am soon going to cut you into pieces and feed you to the evilest of my spirits?" Skell pleaded with Llao; "Will you grant me at least this one wish?"

"Llao felt sure of himself and of his strength, so he released only one of Skells hands. And as Skell reached over to scratch the louse, he grabbed his dagger from within it's sheath, and in one strike, cut off Llao's head and tossed it to the ground."

"The Great Spirit watched this fury between his children and became enraged. This hurt him deeply, because he felt responsible for the destruction the 2 brothers had done to each other. Knowing that there was no other choice, he smote the 3 lovers, which hurt him even more because he loved them so. To honor his children, 3 beautiful mountains arose from their ashes when their bodies fell to the earth."

"Where Loo-Whit-Ka Loo fell, a majestic mountain arose with symmetrical slopes that were blanketed in the whitest of snow. True to her once human form, this beautiful mountain represented her everlasting beauty. To the South of Loo-Whit—Ka Loo, is where Skell fell. The Jagged peaks at the top of the mountain represent him still lifting his head in pride. Llao fell to rest in the north. And even with his warring manor, he still held a tender spot in his molten heart for Loo—Whit-Ka Loo and can still be seen to this day with his head bent in sorrow, weeping to see his beloved forever wrapped in a blanket of wintery snow."

"At first the 3 lovers got along. But soon their warring nature erupted. They began to growl and grumble, stomping their feet so as to spit ash and fire into the air. They belched forth great clouds of black smoke that blocked the sun from the sky. Their tempers flared too much and they began hurling white hot boulders that set fire to the forests and drove the villagers into hiding. Finally, they threw so many stones that it shook the earth so hard it cracked the massive land bridge that held our sacred fire and it crumbled into the river."

"The Great Spirit, being infuriated by his children's careless and selfish behavior; He too shook the foundations of the earth out of anger, causing the mighty river to split and separate each mountain further apart. The Great Spirit then warned his children that they were never to behave in this way again, or else he would destroy their mountains with a tremendous blow."

When the old man quit speaking, he couldn't help but see the panic stricken faces of his fellow medicine men. Trying to find words of comfort, Many Storms finished his tale;

"The reason I have chosen to tell you of this sorrow, is so that you could understand why we fear forming a war party to drive out the white settlers. To anger The Great Spirit can cause terrible destruction. Why should we anger our Spirit Chief by lifting our fists in rebellion, when we know not if they are being sent by The Great Spirit himself?"

The old man paused and began staring into the fire. His tale was over. He had made tell of the destruction life can bring, and knew that it was up to others weather they chose to make the same mistake their ancestors had. Many Storms shifted his weight onto his staff and slowly got up.

"It is time for me to take my leave, but I will share with you with this one last thought; The truth is they have found our land. And no matter if they drive us from our ancestral home; the spirit of our people will never die. It lives in the forests, the rivers and the mountains. It spills over the rocks in the streams and whispers through the trees. We were formed of the earth in which we walk, and our voices will never be silenced."

The deafening silence that followed the tale of the old man's wisdom did not go unnoticed by the group. Or his serene knowledge of life, it was deeply appreciated and not misunderstood. Ever so slowly, just as they had arrived; the men began to disperse until only the original three were left remaining. Spirit Singer was the first to speak;

"I do believe that where ever The Great Spirit places his people that they should be satisfied to remain. They need to be thankful for what he's given them, and not drive others from their own land so they may take it for their own. Just because they perceive our land to be better than theirs, doesn't give them the right to do these horrible things. I shall spend the rest of the evening in prayer, in hopes of having better answers tomorrow."

As Spirit Singer exited the lodge, he couldn't help but think more of what the old man prophesized. He had no previous knowledge of the stories he'd heard tonight. His understanding of the trouble that now faced his people deepened. This was not something that was going to go away. Their way of life was about to change, and for a moment he didn't want to have to be the one to relay this knowledge home.

True to his word, when Spirit Singer returned to his makeshift bed, he dropped to his knees for prayer. Stretching his arms wide and turning his palms face up, he bowed in the direction of the setting sun. After giving thanks to the 4 directions of life, his mind dropped off and his mouth started the rhythmic chant of a seekers guidance.

On the morning of the third day, the elders sent word that they had reached a decision. After everyone gathered in the great lodge, the spokesman arose and stood before the council. He raised his hands and began to speak;

"The council of medicine men have reached a decision. We have decided it is best not to make war against the white man. If his nature is truly as claimed, then he is much like the hornet and if you disturb them, more of them will come. We feel it is best to leave them alone for now."

The Sly One let out a scream of disgust, he spat on the ground and roared;

"Are you frightened women?! Don't you realize the white man will spread out like a great hand! And none of us will be safe from his greedy blood lust? We must stop them now! Before they spread! You said they are like hornets, so let us treat them as such! We can burn them out! This is how you handle hornets!"

The crowd of men whipped into an instant frenzy of shouting approval. The spokesman raised his hands again and in a confident voice, he said;

"We have sent for the Lion Warriors (Chai-Nomo Coo) They will be our eyes and ears. We have given them the position of tribal watchers."

The crowd grew instantly quiet. For the Lion Warriors commanded much respect. Even the pompous Sly One was humbled. Every man knew the fierceness of the Lion Warrior group. They were unmatched in stealth and killing ability.

These men belonged to a fringe cult group that claim the mountain lions spirit as their own. In their right of passage a lone warrior must stalk and kill a lion with only a lance. Then he will perform a ceremony where he takes one of the great cats claw and cut's himself under the left eye. This scaring is proudly displayed as a visual sign of great courage. He will then make a necklace of the fangs and claws and once it is placed around his neck, it will never be removed.

The warrior must then eat the heart of the great cat and ask its spirit to join with his.

The spokesman for the council spoke again and said;

"The decision of the elders stands. Leave the white man alone for now. The Lion Warriors will keep an eye on them. If a lone white man comes too close, he will simply disappear. The Lion Warriors will make sure of this. And if a large group of whites venture to close to your village, we will be warned so we can slip away unnoticed. You can always go back after they have gone."

This concluded the yearly gathering of medicine men. As the men dispersed into the afternoon sun. Spirit Singer gave heartfelt parting words to his friends as he left for home.

Upon his immediate arrival at the village, Spirit Singer informed the elders of the decisions the council of medicine men had made. This resulted in many days of heated debate among the tribal elders. They became uncertain of whether or not they should support the course of action the medicine men were taking. Most of the elders couldn't stand the uncertainty of whether they would have to move or not.

Still Creek (Nowa Aspee-Ah) the oldest member of the elders said;

"Maybe we should avoid this uncertainty and move the village now. Why wait to be forced out? At least this way we can choose the time of our move. For if we have to move in winter, a lot of us old ones will not make it. Each winter it is getting harder and harder for me to get around."

Running Elk (Opo-Wait Na-Saw) one of the other elders, began to speak;

"This is so, and I respect Still Creeks position. But I don't like the idea of uprooting the entire tribe. Not now, this is the best time of year for taking provisions for winter. The streams are full of fish and the deer are plentiful. Are we expected to hunt and dry meats on the move? And which way do we go?

West towards the bitter water, east to the mountain, or further north where it gets colder and the snows stay longer? Who knows, this crazy white man might not even come this way."

Spirit Singer, who had sitting quietly in the background during the days of debate, cleared his throat and motioned to the elders for the permission to speak. For he normally didn't sit in on council meetings, Still Creek nodded to him with a look of curiosity.

"Tribal elders, before you make the decision that can be potentially fatal to every one of us, please let me seek the guidance of The Great Spirit. Maybe I can receive insight on this matter for you. And this will help you make a decision. Give me two weeks to do these things, and hopefully this will give us peace of mind."

Within moments, all the elders agreed in unison to allow Spirit Singer to seek the guidance the tribe so dearly needed.

That night, he told his wife everything that had happened from the time he had left for the medicine man meeting to the council of the elders. She was over whelmed and became frightened. He tried to reassure her by saying;

"We must be strong, help me prepare for the ancient seven day purification ritual.

I will seek guidance as our forefathers did. Black Crow's Daughter asked;

"Have you ever done this before?"

"No, but I have been taught the way. Years ago it was given to me through our tribal history. We have no time to waste, so let us make ready, I will explain as we prepare."

Ten days later, at the end of the ceremony, Spirit Singer felt guided to take his journey east of his village, to the high cliffs of Sacred Mountain. This is an area he had been many times as a youth growing up, and where he felt the closest to The Great Spirit.

Many thoughts went through his mind as he made his way towards the cliffs. For this was also the same area where the sealed entrance to The Great Stone Circle is located. He had passed by it many times on the way to the cliffs.

Upon approaching the rock covered entrance, he stopped and sat down for a rest. Staring intently at the boulders wedged in the ancient cave entrance, he thought to himself;

"It would take ten men days to open this up, if only there was another way in. I would give anything just to see it. Maybe someday if The Great Spirit is willing, I will be granted permission to enter. He must surely know I have dedicated my life to reunite my people with him."

This time, Spirit Singer spoke aloud;

"I'm already in enough agony, I don't need anymore. Stop thinking about such things and move on."

With this being said, he stood to his feet and started up the path towards the cliffs. His physical weakness from the ceremony made it slow going. As late evening approached, Spirit Singer came upon a small plateau over looking the valley of his village. Sitting down, he marveled over the ever changing colors of the settting sun as it gave way to the coming night sky.

Resting his head against the solid rock beneath him, he drifted off to sleep.

Spirit Singer awoke at dawn and began with chants of praise and worship to The Great Spirit. While preparing to rekindle the fire from the night before, he heard odd sounds in the distance coming from somewhere below him. Turning, he slowly scanned the hillside, and there in the dim misty grey light of early morning was a huge hulking figure. Straining his eyes he tried to make out what it could be. Staring intently for several minutes, his worst fears came to life. Raising its head from a patch of huckleberry bushes that clung to the mountain slope, appeared a gigantic brown bear. (Namo Toe—Toe Ma)

Spirit Singer was awe stricken by the shear size of this creature. It was lumbering around grazing on ripe berries. He quickly assessed his options, his back was to the cliffs edge, and for the moment there was no way to get passed the bear. His situation was starting to look pretty hopeless. But after a few moments, he could tell the bear was aware of his presence. This majestic creature just didn't seem to care if he was there or not. Spirit Singer spoke to the bear;

"What are you waiting for? Have you come to kill me? Or are you a messenger from The Great Spirit?"

At the sound of his voice, the bear looked in his direction and began sniffing the air. The bear grunted and then returned his attention to the rotting log he had just found. Tearing it apart with his 6 inch nails, he quickly lapped up the fleeing insects. This shaggy brute was more interested in his breakfast, than the man who now stood before him. Spirit Singer realized that for the moment, the bear had chosen not to take his life. But this could change in less than a heartbeat. He thought to himself;

"If the bear is not here to kill me, then maybe he is a messenger from The Great Spirit. I must wait and watch."

Very slowly, he backed up to the edge of the cliff and quietly sat down and watched this powerful and majestic creature browse for his breakfast. His mind began to fill with many thoughts;

"My people are like this bear, a powerful force to be reckoned with. Each tribe is like the single fingers of one hand. By themselves they are not very strong, but untied and pulled together as a fist, we can deliver a crushing blow. Like this bear, we chose not to kill. To fight or be killed is one thing, to fight or move is another. The wise way is to avoid killing, this is the way of The Great Spirit. So we shall be like this bear. Live our lives in harmony with mother earth. And when danger approaches, we shall slip away before the problems start. Only if there is no way out will we turn and rise up. And like the power of the great bear we will strike back."

As the bear slowly meandered away grubbing and foraging for food, Spirit Singer took this opportunity to gather his things and slip quietly past the bear and back down the mountain.

Back at the village, he arranged for a council gathering with the elders. In his meeting he told them of his insights on the mountain. Still Creek was the first to speak;

"It is wise to listen to these insights. After hearing them, I believe they are good."

The other's nodded in agreement. Their tribe would hold to the decision of the medicine man council. They will avoid the white man for now, and move only if it is necessary.

Later that same day, Spirit Singer was back at his lodge lying by the fire resting, when Black Crow's Daughter approached him smiling and said;
"Now that you have finished your important tribal duties, are you ready for something that will make you happy?"

He took his wife by the hand and pulled her close and said;

"What is that my wife?"

She lovingly held his face in her hands and softly said;

"I am with child."

Surprised, he sat there in disbelief. Then suddenly he leapt to his feet and scooped her up in his arms. Spirit Singer soared with love and laughed with delight. He hugged and kissed her neck and whispered in her ear;

"Does your mother know?"

"Yes, mother is the one who has determined I am with child." She cooed.

"The midwives have also agreed. You shall see your first born in about seven moons."

That night they held each other close, and when she heard his breath become slow and even, Black Crow's daughter was finally able to think about her impending bundle. A pregnant woman often chooses one of the great individuals of her family and tribe as a model for her child. This hero is daily called to mind.

She gathers from tradition all of his noted deeds and daring exploits, and rehearses them to herself when alone. In order that the impression might be more distinct, she avoids company. She isolates herself as much as possible, and wanders prayerful in the stillness of the great woods.

In the passing of time, seasons cycle with no great distinction. One slowly fades as a new one comes into the measure of its strength. Just as with the flame of life, it too will grow dim and die out. But in the fullness of time, life will assert it's self once again.

One morning in early summer, Black Crow's Daughter awoke with the beginnings of labor. The day in which there is to be new life, the miracle of whose making has been entrusted to her was upon her. She and 2 older women set out for a small hut that was located a short distance from the main village.

Spirit Singer was left behind to face the long wait all first fathers go through. Along about mid day, he was joined by his father Blue Hand. Growing concerned about his wife, Spirit Singer said to his father;

"Do you think she is all right? Maybe I should send a woman down to check on her?"

Blue Hand sighed and said;

"One day a rabbit asked a beaver,…How long does it take to stop up a stream? The beaver answered,…As long as it takes." So my son, be patient. It will take as long as it takes. All life is in the hand of The Great Spirit."

Spirit Singer smiled and said;

"Okay father, I'll quit worrying."

Early that evening Spirit Singer heard shrieks in the distance. He went to the lodge door and peered out. One of the old women who was helping his wife was fast approaching. As she passed him he heard her mumbling;

"It's a sign, surely it's a sign!"

Spirit Dreamer motioned for his father to come with him as he stepped out of the lodge, looking for his wife. He finally saw Black Crow's Daughter coming up the trail carrying two small bundles. He couldn't contain himself any longer, he went running to meet her. Standing before her, he breathlessly gazed down awe at the two tiny babies swaddled in her arms. She said to him;

"Look, this must surely be a sign from The Great Spirit! He has given us two baby girls that are the same in every way."

This was very puzzling for him, as he had never ever heard of such an occurrence. And he knew tribal history well enough to know.

Black Crow's Daughter named her little ones Nee—Haish Noe) "Reflections" one name for the two girls. But when she spoke of them or called for them, she said this name twice. So because of this, after a short time, the tribes people started referring to Black Crow's Daughter as Mother Who Calls Twice. (Sai-Om Tettee Too-Ah)

The little girls became a popular topic of conversation among the tribes people. For they all watched with intense curiosity the strange behavior that was exhibited by the two.

As they grew, Reflections stayed to themselves most of the time, and showed very little interest in anyone else. They seemed to know what the other was thinking. And when they spoke, their words would alternate between the two. It was as if they were of one mind and purpose. This behavior made most of the tribes people uneasy. They felt that the girls must have been touched by The Great Spirit in order to act in such a way.

The loneliness the girls faced when it came to socializing with the other children of the tribe didn't seem to bother them. They were happy as long as they were together. The girls never separated from each other. They walked together, they ate together, and they would sing and praise The Great Spirit together. Often, they would sit cross legged in front of one another, as if they were looking in to a mirror and braid each other's hair.

The extreme closeness that reflections shared never bothered Spirit Singer and Mother Who Calls Twice. Years of watching them grow together formed the bond that every parent shares with their child. They accepted them for their very uniqueness and they praised the girls for it.

So it was no surprise When early one morning when the girls were about 14 winters old, Spirit Singer and his wife were abruptly awakened by screams from the girls. Calls Twice rushed to their side to comfort them. They were crying as they recounted their dream aloud;

"Mother, father was riding on the back of a giant brown bear, and he was being chased by a pale and sickly hairy faced man who wanted to kill him! Father was riding as fast as he could trying to get to the village and warn our people! Is he safe?!?

Calls Twice spoke softly;

"Your father is here, and he's all right. It was only a dream. I'm going to stay with you, let us lay down and go back to sleep."

In the morning, Calls Twice told her husband about the strange dream the girls had. He commented;

"I think this is more than a dream. I believe this may have been a vision with a secret meaning. The wisdom of the elders should be consulted."

Spirit Singer wasted no time. He gathered his things and headed for the central meeting lodge. He was granted an audience with the elders almost instantly. During his meeting with the tribal elders, Spirit Singer told of the dreaming vision the girls had.

Still creek, the oldest member of the tribe, pondered the dream for a moment and then began to speak;

"From the time of your daughter's birth, we have all watched them. We've been hoping they have a special purpose in our lives. We've looked for signs that these girls were truly touched by The Great Spirit. We have seen many strange things they do. When they move and speak, it is as if they are one.

and they seem to know each others mind without words. We have given much talk to this matter and we elders believe these girls share the same spirit and are truly a gift to us from The Great Spirit."

"As for their vision, only in the seasons to come will we be able to understand when it's unfolding is revealed. You must be watchful for such things. The other elders and I also feel you must train your girls and cultivate their talents, as a day may come when we will need their gift."

Spirit Singer held to the wishes of the elders and immediately began to educate the girls in the way of the medicine man. He sat down with his girls and said;

"This is the way we begin, above all else remember this; give thanks to The Great Spirit for providing the things we need to live! Be watchful and learn the ways of mother earth. There is an order to all things and you must come to know them well."

This started the training for the two girls. Days rushed by and soon the months turned into a year. Spirit Singer wove an intricate tapestry of details.

He covered everything from chants and prayers to sacred ceremonies of magic.

Mysticism became a way of life for the two. And the sacred trust of the medicine man soon became ingrained in them. As each session ended, they could hardly wait for the next to begin. Day by day the bond created between father and daughters grew into spiritual teacher & his disciples.

One evening, Spirit Singer was gathering some things that he uses when travels. This caught the attention of his daughters. They asked;

"Father, we noticed you're getting ready to travel somewhere. Are we to prepare also?"

"It is almost time for my food offering. This is something I have been doing every fourth new moon since before you two were born. I do it out of respect to my spirit guide the great bear."

The two girls looked at each other and then said;

"This thing you do, is it something we need to learn?"

Spirit Singer smiled and looked into the eager eyes of his loving young daughters. They were breathless with anticipation waiting for his response.

Not wanting to dampen their spirit, he answered;

"Maybe it is time that you go with me on this journey."

He noticed a grave look of concern on his wife's face. He spoke softly to her;

"Don't worry, I would die before I would allow anything to happen to our precious little ones."

Reflections over heard and retorted;

"We are not so little any more!"

Calls Twice lovingly cooed;

"You will always be our babies."

Reflections, wanting to dodge this path of conversation asked;

"What shall we do to prepare father?"

Spirit Singer Replied;

"In a few days it will be the beginning of the new moon. This is the time of my food offering of respect. Years ago when I sought insight from The Great Spirit, I climbed the cliffs at the foot of Sacred Mountain. This is where I was met by a giant brown bear and received my insight. Since that time, on the first day of every fourth new moon, I take an offering to the great bear."

The girls asked;

"What shall we take the bear this time?"

"We shall bring him dried fish and a piece of honeycomb. Bears like nothing better."

Spirit Singer stepped over by the fire and knelt down. His

face took on an eerie amber glow as he looked across the fire with wide eyes at the two girls.

He began;

"When I first started leaving offerings for the bear, I would find a high place where I would be safe. Then I would put my offering somewhere below me, out in the open where I could see it. After this, I would sing the offering chant while beating a small drum."

"The first few years, I would never know when the bear would come. And it wasn't until the next day when I found his tracks did I know he had come. After many winters, now the bear waits close by and listens for the sound of the drum. He is used to me and comes into the open for his offering."

With trembling voices Reflections asked;

"How close have you gotten to the bear father?"

Spirit Singers tone of voice grew stern as he said;

"I always watch from a safe distance. Make no mistake, this bear is a wild and dangerous creature. He could kill a full grown bull elk with one swipe of his massive paw. This is one of mother earths most powerful and majestic animals who rules the mountains and commands much respect."

The girls held each other and shuttered as they spoke;

"We shall always do exactly as you say father. We would

never want to do anything that would bring danger to you or us."

His gentle demeanor quickly returned as he said;

"We will leave for the cliffs in two days."

At dawn on the day of the new moon, Spirit Singer and his daughters set out for the cliffs. They traveled the ancient trail towards the mountain. About a half a day into their journey, Reflections commented to their father;

"How much longer will we have to travel?"

He laughingly replied;

"What's wrong little ones? Getting tired so soon? Do you see the sun where it is now? When it sets low in the sky, but you can still see it, we will be at a place that I like to camp."

With growing concern in their voices, the girls quickly asked;

"Is it safe? Won't the bear find us in the night?"

Spirit Singer paused for a moment and turned back to his girls and looked at them. His heart filled with compassion when he seen the wide eyed expressions. He said;

"Don't worry little ones, it is safe enough. The place of offering is half a days walk beyond the camp."

With a sigh of relief , the girls grabbed their father by the hand and laughingly said;

"We won't get there if you don't stop resting so much!"

He let out a loud growl and began to chase his daughters as they ran ahead of him squealing with laughter.

It was late in the day when they reached the campsite. Spirit Singer began gathering wood for a fire when Reflections asked;

"Father, that place there, over by the big rocks, it looks like the trail goes into the side of the mountain."

He replied;

"It did, many lifetimes ago. That is the old entrance to the cavern of The Great Stone Circle."

The girls, quivering with excitement ran over to their father asking;

"Tell us father, why is it closed up like that?"

Spirit Singer let out a small sigh of sadness remembered and replied;

"After we have eaten and settle in for the night, I will tell the tale of sorrow and what our people have come too."

Later that evening, sooner than planned, he began the story;

"This is the way it was handed down from father to son, generation after generation, and now from me to you. You both know the story of the great medicine man, Joy Of The Soaring Hawk. (Echata Quai Atoke) now I will tell you of a time after his death."

"Several days had passed and Echata had not returned to the village. The elders sent out a search party to look for him. But the only thing they found was his blood stained coat and his medicine bag."

"Months passed, and without a medicine man and spiritual leader, the people became frightened. Soon the elders could ignore the voices of the people no longer."

"The elders spent many days in council trying to figure out what to do. There was no one they could ask, for the last of the builders had already gone on to the other world. And for twenty five winters passing, no one except Echata had been inside the cavern of The Great Stone Circle. For only the guardian was aloud inside after the construction was finished."

"Finally, out of desperation, one man came forth. He was a warrior named Three Wolves. (Kee-Ya Gai-Yomo) he was the second son of one of the builders. It was decided by the elders that they would go into the cavern of The Great Stone Circle, and maybe then they could figure out what to do."

"The elders posted two watchers at the entrance and the rest went into the cavern. As they looked around, one of the men found several drawings on the cavern walls. These were pictures Echata had drawn of his experiences in the cavern. One drawing depicted a man holding the obelisks on The Great Stone Circle. He was surrounded by swirling lines and many faces. The elders didn't quite know what to make of this, but after much talk, Three wolves was chosen to do like the drawings depicted."

"No one really knows what happened next, but the men posted at the entrance said; "We heard what sounded like a mighty rushing wind coming from inside the cavern. It lasted for a short time then it went away with a soft crying sound.

Almost like that of a child in the distance."

"After a long period of silence, the watchers called into the cavern many times. But no one answered. They became worried, so they lit torches and went inside. When they reached the stone circle area, this is what they found. Three wolves was dead, lying in front of The Great Stone Circle. The other men were lying pressed up against the walls of the cavern. They appeared as sleeping, but could not be awakened."

"The men that were alive, were dragged outside. It wasn't until the next day the sleepers were able to wake. Two of the four men said they don't even remember going inside. So whatever happened, scared the memory right out of them."

"Only one man remembered what happened. His name was Stone Bear (No'Cha Toe-Toe-Ma) he spoke very little of what happened. Only that when Three Wolves took hold of the obelisks, the cavern became alive with a storm of rushing wind and flashing blue light, like that of a summer light storm. Then three wolves fell dead."

"Stone Bear was the oldest member of the elders. And it was his decision to seal the entrance to the cavern. He felt that Three Wolves death was a warning, that if they tried this again, it might make The Great Spirit very angry."

The girls were awe stricken by the story. They asked;

"What did they do with Three Wolves?"

Spirit Singer said;

"Nothing. No one wanted to go back in to get him. They felt that what ever killed him, could have him. His bones are still where he fell in front of The Great Stone Circle."

The girls shuttered and drew close to their father. They asked;

"Can we sleep with you?"

He chuckled as he pulled them close and said;
"I'll keep you safe."

Spirit Singer threw more wood on the fire and began unrolling a large elk skin blanket. As he covered his girls, he said;

"It gets a lot colder up here at night."

He then climbed in with the two of them and settled in for the night.

The next morning, Spirit Singer awoke and found himself alone. He quickly sat up and looked around scanning the tree line. "Where are those girls?"

he thought to himself. "They have to be close by." There in the distance, his eyes fixed on to his daughters. "What are they doing?" he mumbled to himself. They were about two stones throw away and off to the side of the trail.

The two girls were standing together and talking and pointing up towards the side of the mountain. Spirit Singer rubbed the sleep from his eyes and wandered over to see what his girls were up too. He called to them;
"What are you two looking at? And WHY didn't you wake me?"

The girls turned and ran to their father. Excitedly they said;

"Father, we had the strangest dream, we were looking to see if it was true!"

"What is that?" He said as he yawned.

The girls began blurting out their dream;

"We kept hearing whispers of many voices, and then they began to call out our name over and over. So we held hands and went looking in the direction of the voices. That way, around to the side of the mountain."

They exclaimed with raised arms as they pointed in the direction they had been.

By this time, Spirit Singer was wide awake and starting to get excited himself. He said;

"Come over here by the fire and tell me more. Take your time and don't leave anything out, no matter if it seems unimportant. This may be a message from the spirits."

The girls took a deep breath and began;

"We walked that way for a while, following the sound of the voices. They grew louder and called to us even more. We came to a place where we had to start climbing. After a while we found ourselves in front of a ledge overhang. And there against the side of the mountain, carved in the stone was the face of a lion with an open mouth. Out of it's mouth came a pale blue light. This was where the voices were coming from. Some how we were not afraid, so we climbed into the mouth of the lion. The blue light became brighter and brighter! Suddenly, we found ourselves in front of The Great Stone Circle. There in the middle stood the spirit of the great Echata Quai Atoke. He spoke to us, he said;"

"My tribal daughters, I have been waiting so long. I am the guardian of The Great Stone Circle. After my death, a warrior came and tried to link with The Great Stone Circle. He was impure and it killed him. So I tell you this, no warrior or taker of life will ever be able to link with us. Only a person of peace that is pure in heart can do this. You two innocent maidens are my chosen ones."

"This is how you can link with us and not be harmed. Stand in front of the obelisk facing each other without touching. Now at the same time, both of you will reach out with one hand and take hold of the one obelisk nearest you. You two share the same spirit and know each others mind. In this way you can spiritually link without becoming physically linked. Doing this in any other way would bring harm to you."

"Now you must ask yourselves this question; are you wiling to do this thing for the sake of our people? If you are, you must be able to give of yourselves with a whole heart. And always yield to the will of The Great Spirit. If you agree to these things, you will be given the charge of guardians of The Great Stone Circle. This act will release my spirit from this place. And I will be able to go back to where all spiritual life began."

"Then we awoke. Father do you think this is real?"

Spirit Singer was amazed. He just sat there with his mouth open. The girls looked at him with wide eyes and said;

"Say something father!"

He took a moment to collect his thoughts and said;

"Please give me time to ponder this dream. While I think on this, let us go and make the food offering. On the way back, we will talk of this more."

Spirit Singer and his daughters made their way up the winding trail to the cliffs. When he came to his place of offering, he set the food on a large flat rock. He then took his girls to a high place of safety. Without saying a word, he took out a small drum from a skin bag that he was carrying. He placed it under his left arm and slowly began to pat the drum. The girls watched their father intently as he began to sway to the rhythmic sound. They knew not to say anything while he was going into a trance like state, for they had seen him do this before.

After a short while, Spirit Singer began to sing. In his song he spoke of many things, the changing of the seasons and the cycles of life, the nature of The Great Spirit and how all things come full circle. Suddenly he dropped his drum and stared off into the sky. One of the girls picked up the drum and continued the rhythmic beat as the other continued to chant. Their father's condition was known as the waking sleep. In this state of mind, he can receive visions from the spirit world.

Spirit Singer remained catatonic for some time. Then, as suddenly as it began, he began looking around. He said to the girls;

"Did you see him?"

They looked at their father curiously and answered;

"See who? The bear?"

Spirit Singer hastily retorted;

"No, No, Echata!"

Reflections looked down and sheepishly said;

"Father, we've seen no one."

He regained his composure and apologized for snapping at his daughters. Then he said;

"I started into my chant like I always do, then I saw a bright blue light and whispering voices! I felt as if I were floating in warm water. Then, there in front of me appeared Echata Quai Atoke, he said to me"

"For the sake of our people, let your daughters come to me, they will not be harmed."

"I told him I could not, for they are young and I fear for their safety."

"He said to me;"

"Then you may come too, but only as a watcher."

"I thanked him and said; "I will do this thing for my people."

As he faded away, I heard him say; "Look for the blue light at night, I await your coming."

"And now I am here."

Spirit Singer grew quiet for a moment, then he said;

"This is not the time or place to be discussing this matter. Let us finish with the offering and get back down to the campsite. We will talk more of it there."

The girls continued the drum beating as Spirit Singer hummed rhythmically. Soon, they heard the sounds of the brush breaking and a snorting low growl. Spirit Singer let out a gasping whisper;

"He is here."

Reflections slowly peered over the edge of the high place they were sitting. There below, coming out of the tangled underbrush was a giant brown bear. He was pushing over small trees as he sniffed the air. Spirit Singer stammered;

"I...I .. have seen this bear many times...But each time I see him, it is like the first."

"I am still amazed at the size of him."

The girls stared with their mouths hanging open. Finally, they squeaked;
"Father, we have no words for this!"

Spirit Singer whispered;

"Sometimes it is best that way."

The bear found his offering and lapped it up in two licks. Then slowly wandered away.

Spirit Singer waited a long while to make sure the bear had gone. Then he and his girls quietly left the area. By the time they were almost to the campsite, it was already getting dark. He said;

"We will stop here and watch the side of the mountain for the blue light."

The girls agreed.

They sat there for a long while until it got completely dark. The quiet of the night was suddenly broken by the girls squealing;

"We see it! We see it! There, just above the tip of that tree!" They exclaimed as they pointed and shook their fingers wildly.

Spirit Singer eagerly joined in;

"Yes, I see it too! We must take turns watching that spot until daybreak. Then we can climb up there and see if it is as revealed to us."

They passed the remaining hours of night talking about the visions they had. Just before dawn, they came to a decision. If they manage to find The Great Stone Circle, Spirit Singer would let the girls link as instructed by Echata.

For the sake of their people, it was worth the risk.

When it became light enough, Spirit Singer and his daughters made their way towards the point of the mountain. By late morning, they reached a position where they could see their camp where they started. In his excitement, he shouted;

"It should be in this area somewhere!"

The girls coming up from behind said;

"Look for the over hanging ledge, the lions face will be below it."

Spirit Singer climbed up on a tall rock and began scanning the side of the mountain. He spotted a ledge overhang not too far from where he was standing. He pointed and shouted to his girls;

"There is one; does it look like the one in your dream?"

The girls made their way over to the overhang. He then heard squeals of excitement. He blurted loudly;

"DID YOU FIND IT!!?!!"

As he impatiently stumbled his way through the rocks towards the girls location. The girls gave a whistling trill of affirmation. As he came up along side his girls, he froze with a fixed gaze. There it was, a massive chiseled face of a mountain lion with an open mouth. It was cracked, weathered and ancient with the ages of many lifetimes ago. The three of them marveled over the masterful piece of work. Spirit Singer commented about the skill and time it must have taken to create such a thing.

Dazed with awe, he felt driven by a surge of spiritual insight. All his fears of what might be faded in the light of what was coming to pass. Here it was, confirmation elements of Reflections dream.

He could tell by the look on his daughter's faces that they wanted to continue this journey as much as he did. He said;

"I feel compelled that we go into the mouth of the lion, but we need to be cautious. Let's make some torches for light and then we will go into the tunnel."

Spirit Singer and his daughters collected their things and returned to the mouth of the lion. They took five large dry pieces of tree limb for torch handles.

Reflections took from their pouch the fire starter materials; flints, dry wood shavings and several swatches of leather that had been soaked in boiling bear fat and bees wax. These were wrapped in tight layers to make the torch heads. Assembling them this way gives a long slow burn time.

All three were trembling with excitement as they lit the first torch. Spirit Singer took a deep breath and said;

"Stay close behind"

He crouched and thrust the torch into the mouth of the lion, then crawled in with the girls in close pursuit, carrying along the extra torches.

It was a slow down grade with shallow turns for the first hundred feet.

Then the tunnel began to gradually widen in width as well as height. Before long they were able to stand. As they continued their downward decent, the tunnel opened up to a honey comb of passages. Spirit Singer stopped to figure out a plan of search. At this point, the first torch was starting to dwindle. He turned to the girls and said;

"Hand me another before this one goes out."

As he began to light the next torch the girls spouted;

"Wait a minute father! Where is that light coming from down there?"

Spirit Singer strained and squinted his eyes as he looked in the direction his daughters were pointing.

"I can't make it out, I've been looking at this torch too long. Hand me the flints just in case it's nothing, and I'll let the other torch go out so I can see."

The torch soon flickered and went out. Leaving only amber glow of red sparks. The smell of burned fat and leather lingered in the air. Both the girls held their noses in protest.

"Give me a few moments girls, the only thing I see now is spots."

He sat down in the suffocating blackness which now engulfed them.

Listening to the sound of each other breathing was his only relief from the feeling of total isolation.

"Give me your hands girls, I need to feel you close. This is unsettling even for me."

They sat there, huddled together for some time before his eyes became adjusted to the dark.

"Can you still see something?"

They answered in unison;

"Yes, over that way."

In frustration, he told the girls;

"I can't tell which way you're looking, grab my head and point me in the right direction."

The girls quickly complied. Spirit Singer squinted and blinked several times, and finally out of the blackness a faint blue light began to appear in the distance.

"I see it now, the pale blue light. Let's keep our eyes on it.

Hold my hand, I'm going to move towards the light slowly, using this torch handle to feel the ground."

They worked their way through the blackness towards the light. The going was painstakingly slow at first. But as they drew closer, the light grew brighter and strangely hypnotic. It seemed to pulse almost like that of a heartbeat.

He felt his way along a smooth rock face that opened up to the main cavern. Abruptly he stopped without saying a word. The girls moved up along side of him;

"What is it father?"

The girls froze in mid step and sentence as their eyes caught sight of the massive open chamber bathed in pale blue light. There in the middle was The Great Stone Circle all aglow with an eerie incandescence. Much like that of a full moon reflecting off the glistening snow on a clear winter's night.

Spirit Singer stammered as he started to speak;

"Don't touch, don't touch anything! And stay close."

They slowly walked into the cavern and made their way over to the front of The Great Stone Circle. Suddenly he jerked and took two quick steps backward. The girls heard a shuttering No!!!! expel from their father's lips. Then he quietly said;

"This must be Three Wolves."

He pointed towards the ground in front of the obelisks of The Great Stone Circle. Laying in a rumpled pile, were human bones and pieces of what looked to be parts of leather clothing. Spirit Singer said to his daughters;

"Let's light a torch so we can see better."

The trio lit up a torch and held it up high. The soft golden light of the torch mingling with the pale blue iridescence created a beautiful life giving green light.

The caverns dusty tomb appearance was transformed as it took on an air of spiritual life force. The fearful caution soon disappeared as they explored the perimeter of the cavern. Reflections said;

"Look father, here on the wall. Drawings, just like you told us."

The three of them stood in awe looking at the group of drawings that were etched there so long ago. Spirit Singer reverently said;

"These were placed here by the hand of the great medicine man, Joy Of The Soaring Hawk. (Echata Quai-Atoke) we must pay respect and honor to his name, and to this holy place. Let us remove the remains of Three Wolves, for this is not a place of burial. Then we will offer up songs of praise to The Great Spirit."

They quickly finished their task and regrouped in front of The Great Stone Circle. Spirit Dreamer began with a chant of praise as his daughters accompanied him with light hearted melody. They chanted and sang as never before. It was magical the way their music echoed around the cavern with the sound of many voices.

As they finished the last of their songs, it seemed to grow strangely quiet.

all three sensed something very odd. It sounded like a low moaning whisper of many voices carried on the wind. And then came a voice very plainly that said;

"You may now link with The Great Stone Circle as foretold...I await."

Spirit Singer gave his daughters a nod of approval. The girls slowly approached the obelisks, and as they did, their minds filled with the chant of evocation. They now stood before the obelisks of The Great Stone Circle, facing one another without touching. In unison they began to speak the ancient chant;

"Of mother earth and father sky, from mighty sun to sister moon. From the east, south, west and north, we call upon brother wind...as gentle as a summer breeze and as strong as a winter storm. For we are they that walked before us, we are the same as a drop of rain or the majestic mountain. For what once was, shall be again!"

With this, they reached out and each girl placed one hand on the obelisk nearest them. Suddenly the sound of many whispering voices came from all directions. The cavern began filling with a rushing wind that swirled around the cavern.

As this was happening, The Great Stone Circle flashed and flickered like a summer lightening storm.

Spirit Singer was frozen with fearful awe. His mind could barely comprehend what his eyes were witnessing. He looked to his girls faces, they were standing there smiling as if nothing was happening. He thought to himself, "They are still alive, and they look happy, so it must be ok." The fearfulness in him gave way to an awesome respect for the power of The Great Stone Circle.

Soon the wind subsided and the flickering light died down to the glow it had in the beginning. The girls then turned loose of the obelisks and stood there somewhat dazed. They walked over to their father and said;

"Are you okay father?"

He stood there dumb founded with his mouth hanging open, he sputtered;

"ME? WHAT ABOUT YOU?!!?"

The girls joyfully blurted in unison;

"Oh father! It was wonderful! Our minds filled with sights and sounds of many lives! And somehow we feel connected to them now. We also talked to the great medicine man who was the first one, Joy Of The Soaring Hawk. He told us many things and a part of him will always be with us. We are sorry we were gone for so many days father."

He looked at his girls with a puzzled frown and said;

"You were not gone anywhere. And you were in the link for only a short while.

Why do you say such things?"

The girls exclaimed;

"Truly father, we went many places and talked to so many people. We spent days and days doing this."

Spirit Singer realized at that moment, the true and mighty power of The Great Stone Circle and the overwhelming responsibility to keep its secrets hidden.

He said;

"Let us go out of this place, I need to think of this more in the light of day."

They took their father by the hand and said;

"We will lead you father, we know the way very well. We don't need the torch light anymore, we have the memories of the builders."

As they started up the passageway, the girls began to explain;

"This passage was made by the builders before they began construction on The Great Stone Circle. It was put here so that fresh air could pass through the cavern. When we try to remember how many times we have been in this place, It's like trying to count the stars in the night sky."

Spirit Singer was amazed at what his daughters were telling him. He said to them;

"This thing we have done is very special. We must keep our coming here a secret. Give me your solemn oath and promise not to tell anyone, not even your mother. This kind of thing would scare her. Give me time to explain to her what has happened."

As they emerged into the light of day, Reflections turned to their father and said;

"We know all to well the importance of what we have done. And if it is not handled properly, this blessing could turn to tragedy. So don't worry father, we promise with our very lives never to reveal our special secret. But first we must tell you about what we've learned. Echata told us of a great many things that are to come our way. Some of which are very bad, father."

"Then we must go and make haste, for if they are as bad as you say, we need time to prepare."

When the three of them left the area, Spirit Singer and his daughters were very cautious to make sure there were no signs that they had ever been there.

Covering their tracks was the most important; Spirit Singer

broke off a branch from the nearby white pine tree and as they departed, he smoothed over all their tracks left in the dirt by lightly "brushing" the ground.

Upon their arrival back at their camp site, Spirit Singer was quick to ask the girls about what Echata had warned them of;

"Girls, I need you to tell me now about everything you and Echata discussed, as I feel we cannot keep our coming here a secret. I will have to inform the tribal elders of your findings. Please start once again at the beginning and please, don't leave anything out."

"Alright father. The first thing he told us about was the white men. Father, he said they are very near! That we don't have much time that our whole land has been taken from us, and we don't even know it! He said that very soon there shall come among us a stranger, speaking an odd language that we don't understand, and he will try to buy our land from us. And Echata told us that we must not sell it!

No matter what they offer, that it's a lie. For if we accept, that they will make us move to an area where no game will live, and the ground will not produce food and there will be no water!"

"Echata then said there will be a messenger from the Suquamish who live on the Whulge. He said you know their Chief, Shaman Si 'Ahl (Chief Seatte). He is to be the spokesman for ALL the tribes. We must leave for home today father.

The messenger is already on his way."

Spirit Singer was plenty shocked by what his girls had told him. But not surprised. He knew the white men were growing all around them. He saw more and more of them every winter. He continually sought council with the elders about the white mans presence, but still his elders decided they should stay.

Spirit Singer was hoping that this messenger was what they needed to make the elders understand that their way of life was about to change forever. And that more of the white men were coming, and there wasn't anything they could do about it.

The trio gathered their things from the campsite, and set out for home with a newly forced urgency. Spirit Singer didn't care that it was almost dark, for he knew the way home very well. It was more important to get back, then wait for the coming dawn. He figured they would reach home just before daybreak.

Just as he'd planned, they entered the village just before dawn. Spirit Singer couldn't help but look around at his beautiful homeland. He couldn't ever imagine leaving here. He silently prayed for a miracle, for if what Echata had told his daughters was right, soon no one would be able to call this "home" anymore.

Upon entering the earthen lodge they occupied, Calls Twice was shocked to see them home so early;
"My husband, what has brought you home so early?

And why did you travel at night? AND WHERE ARE REFLECTIONS?!!"

In unison, the girls called out from behind their father; "We're right here, mother."

Giving a small sigh of relief at seeing her 2 daughters, Calls Twice finally devoted her attention back to her husband;

"And what says you my love?"

"Our journey was cut short due to a sobering vision. I fear to tell you right now, but I shall soon. Reflections and I must leave once again, for we need to seek council with the elders right now. I know not how long this will take, so please be patient, for we will return."

Dropping a kiss to his wife's cheek, Spirit Singer and reflections set out for the tribal elders meeting lodge. Hand in hand the three walked through the center of the village. Reflections was the first to speak;

"Father, we're scared. Will the elders be mad when they find out we linked with The Great Stone Circle?"

"Little ones, the worry is not with the fact you linked with the Circle. The worry lies with what our messenger has to tell us. Fear not what we've done, but what we're about to do. Listen to me when I tell you this, women are not allowed to speak before the council, so I must speak for you. I will need your help if I cannot answer their questions. But do not directly address them, unless they ask you. Standing beside me, we shall unite as one."

The sound of the village dogs barking drew the girls' attention;

"Father, he is here."

Looking west in the early morning sun, Spirit Singer saw a man sliding from the back of a spotted horse. Cautiously the man looked around the village.

He reached into his pouch on his hip and pulled out several pieces of dried meat and tossed it in the direction of the bothersome animals to hush their barking.

Spirit Singer told his girls to go and wait by the lodge while he went and greeted the newcomer. The man noticed him and stopped short in his tracks.

Raising his shield, Spirit Singer saw the emblems painted on the front and knew he was a warrior of the Suquamish tribe. The man quickly addressed him by saying;

"I am here to seek council with the eldest member and spokesman for this tribe. Chief Si' Ahl has sent me to collect the representative and bring him back to our village. The Suquamish and the Du'wamish people are in fear of a war with the white settlers."

Spirit Singer nodded his head in acceptance and led the

man to the elders meeting lodge. Once inside, the spokesman for the council, stood up and spoke;

"I am here to listen to what you have to say young warrior. Please speak."

The young warrior showed no fear as he approached the council. The only noise he made was the clearing of this throat before he spoke;

"Your elders, I pray to The Great Spirit that you may listen to me and heed my words of warning. It has been many moons since we have had contact with each other. During which time, things have changed for our people. The white man has come, bringing more than we can count. They are trying to live among us, but each day they want more and more of our land. Now they are telling us that we are in the way. That they are going to move us to a spot of their choosing and that we are never to leave that place.

"My elders, we have no where left too go. They have conquered every part of our surrounding lands. Our home is now called the United States. And they have a mighty chief that rules and has no respect for our land or our ways. They tell us that we are savage and need to find "their god". They think us to be ignorant because we do not speak as fast as they do. We have tried to tell them that no one owns the land. That The Great Spirit does, and that he allows us to live on it and that no man can ever own the land, sea or air; so I am here before you today, to seek out your spokesman, for he will need to follow me to the meeting of the white men as your representative."

Still Creek, the eldest member of the tribe, motioned to the council spokesman that he was no longer needed. Wearily the old man rose to speak to the warrior;

"We have been aware of the white man for sometime. And we do not wish to lose our home to these "flies" that do not go away when swatted. But we do not want bloodshed and we have been against a war from the beginning. So I will send our medicine man Spirit Singer and his 2 daughters to this meeting. Maybe he can talk your chief out of starting a war, for we are but a few, and they are a great many."

The young warrior accepted his answer and began scanning the lodge for his 3 new companions. Spirit Singer immediately stepped forward and asked the council to speak;

"Elders, I ask that I may speak to you, for my daughters and I knew of this messenger, even before he arrived."

Still Creek nodded, allowing Spirit Singer to continue;

"As per your request, I have been teaching my daughters the ways of the shaman and medicine man. So it was of necessity that I took them with me on my journey to pay respect to my Spirit Guide, the great bear. During which time I was contacted in a vision quest by the great medicine man, Joy of the Soaring Hawk.

He asked my permission for my daughters to link with The Great Stone Circle. So we ventured east to sacred mountain, where he showed us another entrance into the cavern. I was allowed to go in, but only as a watcher. For only Reflections were allowed to touch The Great Stone Circle. They were only in the link for a short time, but to them, it was many days. Joy of the Soaring Hawk chose Reflections as his replacement. He warned them of the messenger that stood before you, so it is without fear, but with a heavy heart that I will accept my mission."

Still Creek crept forward to speak to Spirit Singer;

"We are happy to learn that our people have finally reconnected with The Great Spirit. But we are also saddened by the circumstances in which followed.

We wish to hear more of this topic when you return from the Whulge."

Spirit Singer motioned for the warrior to meet him outside. When they gathered outside, he asked the warrior when they were to leave;

"You spoke of an urgency in returning to your people, so when do we leave for our journey?"

"I fear you do not understand my brother, we should have left already."

"Please allow me a very short amount of time to gather some food for our travel."

"We can also hunt on our way, but I understand your need. I will meet you outside your lodge shortly."

Arriving at his lodge with his 2 daughters in tow, Spirit Singer quickly told his wife Calls Twice that they are leaving again. She put up some protest, but it was quickly quelled as he hugged her goodbye and grabbed his camp pack he'd dropped off earlier. Reflections followed their father's instructions, and within moments they were already heading west towards the snow capped mountains.

The journey was rough going at first. As the terrain in which they travelled was rocky and steep. The valley in which they lived was far separated from the outside world. This would be the first time Reflections had ever ventured over the westward mountains that surrounded their lush valley home. Unaccustomed to riding horses, the girls clung closely together when their father led their horse up the rocky path.

After 2 days of constant traveling they reached the newly founded Washington Territory that surrounded the Whulge. The girls were in awe of the mighty buildings that seemed to be everywhere. They were shocked by the lewd crass behavior of these pale faced men who stumbled about like they were dizzy.

They knew not what they said but could tell they were shouting at them like a dog. Spirit Singer quickly whisked his girls off their horse and into the safety of a shelter the warrior had led them too.

Startled by the commotion that he was unaccustomed too, Spirit Singer asked the warrior when the meeting was to take place;

"I am anxious to get this meeting over with, can you tell me when the meeting is going to take place?"

"We are waiting for the White governor, it is said he is to arrive anytime now on a ship the likes you've never seen. He is to negotiate the sale of our lands, for they have told us we no longer have a choice."

"Please find comfort in this place, for I see your daughters and you, are in need of rest. When the ship arrives, I will fetch you and your daughters."

As Spirit Singer unrolled is pack for himself and his daughters, he couldn't get over the loud noise that was coming from the outside. He thought it to be music, but was unsure. He never realized until that moment, just how much trouble their way of life was in. Reaching over, he pulled his daughters close to find the comfort he needed and finally fell into a deep sleep.

The sound of a horn and many drums awakened the slumbering trio;

"Father! What is that noise?!"

"I believe the white Governor has arrived, my little ones."

Gathering their things, they spoke very little. Spirit Singer had no words of comfort for his trembling daughters. He could only caution them as to stay close to his side and not to look any white man in the eyes. A few moments later the warrior appeared and summoned them to follow. Wrapping themselves up in their elk skin blankets, they followed the warrior without complaint.

PART 3
The Chiefs

It was a cold December day in 1855 on the shores of the Whulge. Over a thousand Indians had gathered to await the arrival of the ship carrying the new white governor. Spirit Singer and his daughters had never seen so many Indians gathered in one place. They knew very little about this man, only that he carried their fate in his hands.

The elk skin clad newcomers kept their vigil on the wintery shores awaiting the white governor named Isaac Stevens. Finally the anchor dropped and the new governor stepped ashore without ceremony. He was a diminutive man, brusque in his manner and direct in his approach to people and problems. He had been appointed to facilitate the settling of the area, and to do so, in his mind meant he had to remove all the natives so they would not impede the progress of the white settlers. He was very anxious to get on with the matter.

He began speaking in such fast sentences, that even the interpreters were hard pressed to understand. Little was understood by the Indian people, except this man intended to remove them from their ancestral lands and place them on prison plots called "reservations."

When the funny little man stopped speaking, the Indians turned toward Chief Si' Ahl, (Seattle). He was recognized as the leader of the allied tribes. And it was only natural that he should speak for them all. Si' Ahl knew that the haughty little man who had emerged from the ship represented the end of the Indians' dreams and visions of free people.

So it was with a sense of sadness, mixed with no little contempt and scorn, that Si' Ahl rose to speak in response to the new governor. He chose his words carefully, and in the Indian way, he spoke clearly and from the heart;

Yonder sky that has wept tears of compassion upon my people for centuries untold, and which to us appears changeless and erternal may change. Today is fair. Tomorrow may be overcast with clouds.

My words are like the stars that never change. Whatever Si' Ahl says, the Great Chief at Washington can rely upon with as much certainty as he can upon the return of the sun or the seasons.

The White Chief says that the Big Chief at Washington sends us greetings of friendship and goodwill. This is kind of him, for we know he has little need of our friendship in return.

His people are many. They are like the grass that covers our vast prairies.

My people are few. They resemble the scattered trees of a storm swept plain.

The Great Chief sends us word that he wishes to buy our lands, but is willing to allow us enough to live comfortably.

This indeed appears just, even generous, for the red man no longer has rights that he need respect. And the offer may be wise also, as we are no longer in need of an extensive country.

There was a time when our people covered the land as the waves of a wind ruffled sea cover its shell-paved floor. But that time long since passed away with the greatness of tribes that are now but a mournful memory.

I will not dwell upon, nor mourn over, our untimely decay, nor reproach my white brothers with hastening it, as we too may have been somewhat to blame.

Youth is impulsive. When our young men grow angry at some real or imaginary wrong, and disfigure their faces with black paint, it it denotes that their hearts are black, and that they are often cruel and relentless, and our old men and old women are unable to restrain them.

Thus it has ever been. Thus it was when the white man first began to push our forefathers westward.

But let us hope that the hostilities between us may never return. We have everything to lose and nothing to gain.

Revenge by young men is considered gain, even at the cost of their own lives. But old men who stay at home in times of war, and mothers who have sons to lose, know better.

Our good father at Washington—for I presume he is now our father as well as yours, since King George has moved his boundaries further north—our great and good father, I say, sends us word that if we do as he desires, he will protect us. His brave warriors will be to us a bristling wall of strength, and his wonderful ships of war will fill our harbor so that our ancient enemies far to the northward—the Haidas and the Tshimshian—will cease to frighten our women, children, and old men.

This in reality will he be our father and we his children.

But can that ever be?

Your God is not our God. Your God loves your people and hates mine. He folds His strong protecting arms lovingly about the white man and leads him by the hand as a father leads his infant son. But He has forsaken his red children—if they are really His.

Our God, The Great Spirit, seems also to have forsaken us. Your God makes your people wax strong everyday. Soon they will fill all the land. Our people are ebbing away like a rapidly receding tide that will never return.

The white man's God cannot love our people or He would protect them. They seem to be orphans who can look nowhere for help.

How then can we be brothers? How can your God become our God and renew our prosperity and waken in us dreams of returning greatness?

If we have a common heavenly father He must be partial— or He came to his white children. We never saw Him. He gave you laws but had no word for His red children whose teeming multitudes once filled this vast continent as the stars fill the firmament.

No, we are two distinct races with separate origins and separate destinies. There is little in common between us.

To us, the ashes of our ancestors are sacred, and their resting place is hallowed ground. You wander far from the graves of your ancestors, and seemingly without regret.

Your religion was written upon tablets of stone by the iron finger of your God so that your could not forget. The red man could never comprehend nor remember it.

Our religion is the traditions of our ancestors—the dreams of our old men, given them in the solemn hours of night by The Great Spirit, and the visions of our sachems—and is written in the hearts of our people.

Your dead cease to love you and the land of their nativity as soon as they pass the portals of the tomb and wander way beyond the stars. They are soon forgotten and never return.

Our dead never forget the beautiful world that gave them being.

They still love its verdant valleys, its murmuring rivers, its magnificent mountains, sequestered vales and verdant-line lakes and bays, and ever yearn in tender, fond affection over the lonely hearted living, and often return from the Great Beyond to visit, guide, console, and comfort them.

Day and night cannot dwell together. The red man has ever fled the approach of the white man, as the morning mist flees before the morning sun.

However, your proposition seems fair and I think that my people will accept it and will retire to the reservation you offer them. Then we will dwell in peace, for the words of The Great White Chief seem to be the words of nature speaking to my people out of dense darkness.

It matters little where we pass the remnant of our days. They will not be many. The Indians' night promises to be dark. Not a single star of hope hovers above this horizon.

Sad-voiced winds moan in the distance. Grim fate seems to be on the red man's trail, and wherever he goes he will hear the approaching footsteps of his fell destroyer and prepare stolidly to meet his doom, as does the wounded doe that hears the approaching footsteps of the hunter.

A few more moons, a few more winters—and not one of the descendants of the mighty hosts that once moved over this broad land or lived in happy homes, protected by The Great Spirit, will remain to mourn over the graves of a people once more powerful and hopeful than yours.

But why should I mourn at the untimely fate of my people? Tribe follows tribe, and nation follows nation, like the waves of the sea. It is the order of nature, and regret is useless.

Your time of decay may be distant, but it surely will come.

For even the white man, whose God talked with him as friend with friend, cannot be exempt from the common destiny.

We may be brothers after all. We shall see.

We will ponder your proposition and when we decide, we will let you know. But should we accept it, I here and now make this condition, that we will not be denied the privilege without molestation of visiting at anytime the tombs of our ancestors, friends, and children.

Every part of this soil is sacred in the estimation of my people.

Every hillside, every valley, every plain and grove, has been hallowed by some sad or happy event in days long vanished.

Even the rocks, which seem to be dumb and dead as they swelter in the sun along the silent shore, thrill with memories of stirring events connected with the lives of my people. And the very dust upon which you now stand responds more lovingly to their footsteps than to yours, because it is rich with the blood of our ancestors and our bare feet are conscious of the sympathetic touch.

Our departed braves, fond mothers, glad, happy hearted maidens, and even our little children who lived here and rejoiced here for a brief season, will love these somber solitudes, and at eventide they greet shadowy returning spirits.

Let him be just and deal kindly with my people. For the dead are not powerless.

Dead, did I say? There is no death. Only a change of worlds.

Upon completion of Chief Si' Ahl's magnificent heart moving speech, the white governor turned away from him and boarded his ship. No other words were spoken. Chief Si' Ahl then walked away and disappeared into the crowd. Spirit Singer looked to the warrior for help. But the warrior had none to give. He then turned to his daughters and said;

"We must leave for home now. I am sorry to make you travel so far, but we have no choice. Chief Si' Ahl has spoken and it seems there is little for us to do here. Let us leave this place for now, and hope we shall never have to return."

The girls agreed and couldn't wait to leave the now bereft, trodden upon Whulge the Suquamish once called their home.

The travel home was not as hurried as before. Spirit Singer had no desire to relay to the elders what had become of the Suquamish Indians. Or for that matter, what was in store for them. He had found himself in this position once before, long ago before his girls were born. He sought the help of The Great Spirit, and ended up finding his Spirit Guide. So maybe this is what he must do?

He was unsure of his next course of action, for he knew how stubborn the elders could be. And with winters coming being felt once again, he knew they would not want to move the tribe and head east past sacred mountain. But sadly, even if they did move, how long would they be safe? How many seasons would pass before they would be discovered hiding? The new Great Chief in Washington may not look kindly upon them.

Spirit Singers heart ached with indecision and apprehension. He could think of nothing else all the way home. Even when they camped at night, he stayed to himself saying little to his lonesome daughters. Spirit Singer finally succumbed to the fact that they had no choice. It was either move on there own, or be forced to move where ever the white governor decided to put them. At least he now had a plan, and knew what he needed to get the elders do.

***

Calls Twice was overjoyed when she saw her family approaching. She shrieked with joy and ran down to greet them. Reflections crowed around their mother telling her how much they had missed her. Broken in spirit and dirty, they willingly followed their mother home while Spirit Singer went straight to the lodge of the elders as he was instructed to do. Home life was going to have to wait this time. Sadden and dismayed, Spirit Singer approached the lodge of the elders.

As he entered the lodge, he heard a fellow villager complaining of another.

And upon the elders seeing Spirit Singer, the fellow villager was dismissed and told to return tomorrow.

When all had left the lodge that wasn't included in the

council, Spirit Singer dropped to his knees in front of the council and began to speak;

"My elders, what I have seen and heard was an awful sight. I kneel before you today begging you to listen to me. It is true what the warrior has said. Our way of life is changing rapidly. We will not have anywhere to go, if we don't leave now. For if we stay, we will be moved by the white man and his Chief, we will be forced to live on what they call "reservations". We must go now, when we can escape their prison they have waiting for us. The only direction that we can go is east, past sacred mountain and onto the prairies. But it will only hold them off for a while, as the white man has conquered and destroyed our land in every direction. The Whulge is gone, it is now a white mans city."

After a few moments of thought, the tribal elders spoke;

"Spirit Singer, we trust what you say, but we need to discuss this matter in private. We will send for you when we've reached a decision. Thank you for your words, they have been heard. Go in peace and enjoy your family."

Walking away, Spirit Singer couldn't help but wonder to himself why they had dismissed him so easily. They didn't ask him to elaborate more on the situation and they certainly didn't offer any clues to as how they are going to rule on the matter. He guessed he would have to leave it up to The Great Spirit.

The weariness of his travels finally took ahold of him when

he reached his lodge. He was happy to see that Reflections had already fallen asleep. They had been through much this past moon. So without much further thought, Spirit Singer drifted off into a deep slumber.

Morning time came and Spirit Singer eagerly awaited a response from the elders. By midafternoon, still nothing. Evening came and went, and still nothing; the uncertainty of the situation was agonizing for him. He knew that every day they deliberated, the white men were gaining ground. They didn't have any time to waste, and smoking their medicine pipes filled with Kinni'Kinnicki didn't appear to be doing any good; for they would have seen a vision by now. Spirit Singer suspected that the old ones of the tribe were being the most stubborn. They didn't fear the white man. They feared no one.

As the days passed and he was never summoned to the council, Spirit Singer realized that the elders must not of been able to agree. So with much regret, Spirit Singer and his daughters continued their life as if their trip to the Whulge had never happened.

When the January snows arrived, piling themselves in drifts, they also brought along another visitor to the village. This one, no one knew was coming.

Spirit Singer was on his morning rounds of the village with his daughters when in the distance, they saw what looked to be a small campfire burning itself out on the outskirts of their village. Confusion turned to curiosity so they decided to go investigate the happening.

Nothing could have prepared them for what they saw when they reached the smoldering fire. It was a small boy, about 8 winters old. He was badly injured and had bled profusely throughout the night. Pools of frozen coagulated blood were stuck like ice to the tiny blanket the boy was laying on. Spirit Singer and his daughters rushed to his side to see if he was still among the living. Upon close inspection they determined he was breathing, but very slow and shallow. His frozen blanket made an awful ripping sound as Spirit Singer plucked the boy from his makeshift bed, leaving behind patches of frozen earth that clung to the underside of the stiff blanket.

Spirit Singer rushed the boy to their lodge. Quickly they piled blankets over his frozen form and laid him next to the fire. He then backed away and sat down by his daughters. Speaking out loud but to no one, he voiced his thoughts;

"How did this boy come to be laying half dead outside his village? The child didn't live here, for their village was small enough that he knew all the children. But where could he have come from? The nearest village was…No, it couldn't be! How could a Suquamish child make it here by himself? There were no other tracks by the boys camp. Only his made from the night before."

"I just don't understand this, girls. We had better do everything we can to keep this boy alive, even though my gut is telling me that nothing good will come of this."

When the boy's skin was warm to the touch once again, Reflections uncovered him enough to dress his wounds. He had a small hole in his side that went straight through him. There was no arrow or lance stuck inside. It was like something burned his insides as it went through him. They had never seen a wound such as this. They called for their father to help them. After he looked at the wound, words replayed in his head of what other medicine men had told him.

He remembered them saying that the white men had sticks made of thunder that would leave holes like this. And just as he had thought, he said it aloud again;
"Nothing good will come of this, I hope he lives."

The hours passed by and the afternoon was replaced with the chilly winter night. Spirit Singer had delegated himself as the boy's watcher. And sometime late into the night, the boy started to move on his own as he became conscious.

The crackling of the fire startled the boy and he began thrashing about wildly.

"CALM YOURSELF young one!" Spirit Singer said.

"You are safe, here in the village of The Stone Circle People. Why are you here alone? Where are your parents?"

Choking out a dry raspy cough, the boy reached for the satchel of water that lay by his side. After several long pulls on the water, the boy responded;

"You say I am in the village of The Stone Circle Tribe? Then that means I made it!"

Grunting in pain from his over animation, the boy went on;

"My father told me to head East, in the direction of the rising sun for 2 days and I would find your village. He said he knew a man and his 2 daughters that lived here and that it would be a safe place for me to stay."

"Boy, is your father one of the Suquamish warriors?"

"Yes, he was."

"What do you mean…was?"

"My father was killed in a great war that was started by us. The new white governor said he was tired of dealing with us Indians, so he put a price on our head of 5 gold pieces."

"Do you know how long ago this war was and if they won?"

"We didn't win. My father was killed when he attacked the white man that scalped my mother. The war only lasted 1 day. They killed most of us, and who they didn't kill, they placed in what they call a "Jail". I think this happened 5 nights ago."

"You get some more rest boy. We will speak of this more tomorrow."

Spirit Singer was relieved that the boy lived, but also saddened to hear what happed. So it was true, thought Spirit Singer. The white man does intend to take all of our land. And he is coming this way.

The next morning, Spirit Singer made the decision that he and his daughters were going to seek the guidance of The Great Spirit from The Great Stone Circle. He had thought it through the night before, and realized that it is up to him to save the tribe. So he will go against the elders, for they are not responding. Today they will leave for sacred mountain.

Spirit Singer hated to rouse his sleeping daughters, but he had no choice.

Now more than ever did the tribe need guidance, and his daughters were the only ones who could do it. Quietly they packed their bedrolls, gathered their food supply and slipped out the door. Turning back, Spirit Singer stopped a moment and laid his hand on his wife's cheek, tenderly he said to her; "My heart longs for the time when we shall see each other again. Love you wife." He then disappeared down the trail.

Catching up with his daughters, he cautioned them to be careful, because if a small boy could make it this far, other people may have also. The land is no longer free and untamed, who knows what they could run into on their way.

On towards the middle part of the day, when the sun was at its highest point in the sky, they decided to sit and make a fire to warm themselves. Their fur lined moccasins needed a little more bear fat applied to the outsides anyway.

The water was starting to seep through the grease and get their feet wet. Luckily, it hadn't snowed last night, so the travel was easy. They continued on with their journey after a light snack of dried buffalo meat.

They reached their campsite a little while before dark. Spirit Singer had to act quickly to get the rocks hot enough to heat the ground. This was a way they kept warm when out in the winter conditions. They would make a small fire and put rocks in it, they would then dig out a depression big enough for themselves, and place the rocks deep inside. They would then cover it back up with dirt and lay their blankets on top. This would keep the ground slightly warm, so they didn't freeze to death in their sleep.

It was slow digging, as the dirt was very frozen, but he made enough of a depression that the rocks could sit nicely inside. After throwing the blankets down, Spirit Singer slid inside to make sure it wasn't too warm. He thought to himself, "yep, just as he thought, just right."

The girls quickly jumped in next to their father. Between the warm rocks and their combined body heat, they should be warm until daybreak.

Soft tickles of newly fallen snow floated softly to rest on the girls' faces rousing their slumber. The sun had just started to rise in the east giving an orange and red glow to their wintery surroundings when they realized they were alone. Looking around, the girls began searching for their father. It only took two steps and the girls found him, crouched behind a boulder. Reflections had just started to open her mouth when her father's hand was fast extended to stop her impending speech. Slowly he lowered his hand to motion for them to sit quietly.

Doing as they were commanded, the girls hugged one another, for they knew something was terribly wrong.

Slower than the girls had ever seen, their father crept backwards towards them. Extending his arm across their chest he pushed them along with him. They rounded the edge of their temporary camp and Spirit Singer softly whispered;

"Shhhhh.. Don't say anything, someone has found us. He is hiding just over yonder. Our campfire drew his attention in the night. I heard his feet echoing lightly in the snow while we were sleeping. When I moved, he disappeared and hasn't shown himself since. I've kept an eye on that spot since before dawn. He cannot follow us. I fear he is a scout. We are going to have to take a different way home that will confuse him. Hopefully he will become lost in the snow. Try not to make a sound, and do exactly as I do."

Reflections nodded quickly to their father and soundlessly gathered their packs.

Spirit Singer knew that it would be tough to hide their tracks in the newly fallen snow. And in the back of his mind, he hoped they wouldn't have to fight this man. Spirit Singer had never taken a life, but he would have no choice if this pest didn't stop following them.

Scanning the countryside, Spirit Singer looked for any tracks they might have left in the snow from the night before. Satisfied with the outcome of his search, Spirit Singer instructed his daughters on how to walk and which way he wanted them to go. The idea he had was that if they made lots of tracks in the snow, that this stranger wouldn't be able to follow them. They went back and forth and over rocks and walked along fallen trees, only to end up back where they were. He had the girls walk in opposite directions, hoping he'd choose the wrong path. Spirit Singer knew that he only needed to do this until they reached sacred mountain, for the cliffs would hide them well. Spirit Singer knew that it was a childish attempt to hide themselves, but he had no other option. The man already knew they were there.

Spirit Singer deduced that if the man wanted to kill them, he'd of done so while they were sleeping. No, this man was smart. He kept on their heels every step of the way.

Cautiously they climbed the icy mountain slopes, following a small trail made by animals, careful not to make any noise that would disrupt the heavy ice glazed snow. Spirit Singer and his daughters had just reached a rocky outcrop above the tree line, when a reverberating boom of a Hawkens 50 Caliber Muzzleloader (the white mans thunderstick) echoed off the surrounding mountain tops, penetrating the muffled silence of the wintery landscape. The deafening noise shook the loose snow right off the nearby tree limbs.

An overwhelming panic raced through Spirit Singer. He knew the white man was shooting at them. They were trapped, no where to go but up. He ushered the girls closer to him. Crouching behind a twist in the trail he assessed the situation. He had no choice but to try and lead the man away from his daughters, which meant he had to leave them here on the side of the mountain.

But it would be better to leave them to their own accord, than have this white man scalp them for the bounty of 5 gold pieces.

Spirit Singer had no time to waste, so he hugged his daughter's goodbye and slid feet first over the edge of the outcrop. Sliding down the mountain he began dodging the small trees sticking out of the snow. The warmth of his body melted the snow that clung to his clothes and within moments he felt the icy chill creep over his skin. Half numb, he thrust his feet to the side to stop himself against the stump of a tree. Looking up he could see his daughters no more, and silently sent his wishes of love.

A low moaning guttural growl broke through his thoughts. Spirit Singer quickly looked around as the hair on the back of his neck stood on end, and his stomach started to churn when not more than 20 feet in front of him appeared a winter lethargic ridden brown bear. Choking back a sob of fear, he laid motionless in the snow while the bear swayed back and forth displaying his awesome size.

The bear reared back and began sniffing the air emitting gusts of steam out of his nose in big bursts with every breath.

Dropping to his haunches, the bear turned his head in the opposite direction. Something else caught his attention. Grateful for the reprieve, Spirit Singer tried to form a plan. For now he had to escape two life threatening obstacles. When the bear shifted his attention, he noticed something oddly familiar. The fact that it didn't attack him immediately was very puzzling. Even in the bear's lethargic state, he knew he didn't have a chance at evading him. He only hoped the bear would be drawn away by the white mans scent.

This time the boom of the muzzleloader was even more deafening than before as it wedged its tiny cannon ball into the tree above Spirit Singer's head.

Scrambling through the snow he tried to hide himself from the white man and the bear. He could find no shelter, and the bear was even more disturbed by the thunderous boom. The bear snarled and worked himself up into a frothy mess.

Bits of saliva dripped off his snarling mouth as he growled and snorted and pawed the ground.

The next shot was right on target. It hit the enormous bear in the shoulder.

He let out a howl of pain as the cannon ball drove itself deep into the meat of the shoulder blade. Spirit Singer was forgotten at the moment by the bear, so he edged closer to see if there was away around the onslaught of cannon balls being shot as fast as the white man could repack the muzzle of his weapon. Spirit Singer figured it took the white man only about 25 beats of his heart before he fired another shot.

Observing the bears outward displays, Spirit Singer could tell that he was about to charge the white man and rip him to tattered shreds with his enormous paws. As he edged closer to the bear, his nostrils filled with the smell of mossy dirt mixed with the lingering scent of raw salmon that clung to the animal's fur. His heart raced and he timed his jump, he knew he only had one chance. When the bear moved forward to charge his assailant, Spirit Singer leapt forward and grabbed a hold of the bear's fur and propelled himself atop the bear. He paid no attention to him, for the bear was intent on charging the small white man with a hairy face.

Spirit Singer wrapped his arms around the bear's thick furry neck and ducked his head to the side. One more shot rang out, echoing around him. The bear stumbled and lost his footing. Spirit Singer still held on, until the bear toppled and rolled over onto him, pinning him to the ground. He felt the bones in his chest crush beneath the weight of the massive bear. He couldn't breathe, the air in his chest felt like thick liquid as the weight of the bear forced him to expel the last of his breath.

Shrill screams sliced through the stillness in the air. Dazed and unable to breathe, Spirit Singer knew that it was his twin girls screaming from above. They didn't listen to him. They didn't leave as he'd instructed. The sound of snow crunching under heavy steps captured his attention. Barely able to lift his head, Spirit Singer saw the hairy white man approaching him. The barrel of his hefty gun was pointed right at his chest. The white man began speaking to him like he was supposed to understand what he was saying. His words were muffled by the loud ringing in his ears. Closing his eyes, he gave himself up to The Great Spirit as the last shot rang out. Petrified, the girls couldn't tear themselves away. They knew their father was dead.

They watched in horror as the white man then proceeded to pull a shiny knife from his side and grab a handful of their father's silver streaked hair and in one motion, scalped it clean to the bone.

The girls unable to watch the horrifying scene any longer dragged themselves away from the edge of the outcrop. Stumbling and crying they couldn't see where they were going through the tears in their eyes. It seemed to blur their vision and their mind. They could barely remember what their father had told them to do. Somehow they found the courage and strength to move on, they didn't care if they left tracks in the snow or not. All they could think of was finding somewhere safe to hide.

The Great Spirit looked kindly upon them that cold January day. For the white man didn't seem to be pursuing them. It seemed he accomplished what he had wanted and chose not to follow the girls up the side of the mountain. The girls were unaware of the white mans decision, so they continued climbing the trail until they reached the face of the lion. Looking around, they paused before they entered the mouth. Shaking, they held each other's hands and entered the cavern.

Once inside the cavern of The Great Stone Circle, the girls lit one of the torches that lined the perimeter of the cavern. They gathered what remained of some wood that was left there lifetimes ago and striking a fire, the girls huddled close and spoke not a word. Silently they huddled until the waves of shaking stopped. Reflections looked at one another and they both rose, walking towards the Stone Circle they reached out their arms to make the link. The pale blue light began strobe and flash like lightening, the hurricane winds rushed at them from all 4 directions blowing their clothing apart and sweeping their hair from their heads. It circled the cavern and blew out their fire. The intensity of the noise in which the Circle grumbled and groaned was tremendous. Frightened by the display, the girls still hung on. They looked into each others eyes and in the loudest voice they could muster, they began speaking the chant in unison;

"OF MOTHER EARTH AND FATHER SKY, FROM MIGHTY SUN TO SISTER MOON, FROM THE EAST, SOUTH, WEST AND NORTH WE CALL UPON YOU BROTHER WIND! GENTLE AS THE SUMMER BREEZE AND STRONG AS THE WINTER STORMS! BREATHE UPON US THE INSIGHT OF THE GREAT SPIRIT! FOR WE ARE THEY THAT WALKED BEFORE US! WE ARE THE SAME AS A DROP OF RAIN, OR THE MAJESTIC MOUNTAIN! FOR ONCE WHAT WAS SHALL BE AGAIN!!!"

***

When Reflections turned loose of the obelisks, their hands were bleeding from the force in which they gripped them. Dazed from the life forces that had travelled through their body the girls slowly turned around and saw their father standing before them in spirit form. His hollow voice beckoned them to him;

"Do not worry my little ones, I am still here. The things I know, I cannot tell you, but I wish I could. You must find them out on your own. So you must leave this place, and hide it well. For the white men must not find our link, or else he will destroy it like everything else they touch. They do not understand our ways.

Please be safe on your journey, you no longer need to worry about the white man who took the life of my mortal body. He did not make it too far before the Lion Warriors caught him. Remember girls, I will always be here, waiting for you."

"We love you father, we will miss you terribly."

Like a wisp of smoke, their father vanished into the air. Trembling they dropped to their knees and crawled over to their now cold and ashen fire. Looking at each other they realized they no longer needed to speak words between them.

They could hear what the other was thinking simply by looking at her. Reflections looked at her sister and said;

"You're right, it is time for us to go."

Out of the mouth of the lion they came, leaving behind the sadness they had when they entered. They were of one mind and purpose. No white man was going to take their lives, or the lives of their people any longer. The Great Spirit put us here first. This was our land, they could go back to own. And after they buried their father's body with the heart of his spirit guide the big brown bear, they would begin yet again, another journey.

The masticated carnage that beheld their eyes when they reached the devastated remains of their father was almost intolerable. They arrived only to find that many animals had taken a meal or two from their father and his spirit guides remains. The snow surrounding the bodies was nothing but a red mush.

Many animals had feasted a plenty, leaving behind their tracks in the bloody snow.

Reflections gagged as they pulled hard on the now frozen remains of their father, dislodging it from underneath the half eaten bear. They tied some branches together with strips of their clothing to make a plank on which to place their father. After which they wedged the plank up high in a nearby tree and laid their father to rest. Reflections then returned to the big brown bear and thanked him for his courage. They then cut into his half frozen chest and removed his heart and placed it aside their father to keep him company on his journey into the spirit world.

Leaving their much loved father behind, Reflections headed south to the village of the Chute—Pa—Lu (Nez Perce). Upon which they are to find their Chief In-Mutt-Too Yah—Lat-Lat (Thunder Traveling Over Mountains). There they were told they would find the answers they seek.

Reflections checked a tree to see which side the moss was growing on and relied upon that to tell them which way to travel. Moss only grows on the north side of trees, so the opposite way would be south. Gathering their things, the girls checked their direction again, and headed south. They couldn't help but notice the clouds in the sky, warning them of an impending storm. Reflections picked up their pace and headed the southerly direction.

Late in the day, Reflections stopped to check the food provisions Calls Twice had sent with them. The food was almost gone. Luckily, neither one of them felt much like eating. But their bodies needed fuel to keep warm, as the winter weather was wearing them down. They split the last of their dried jerky and sipped some water, and continued on until the sun reached the lowest point in the sky. They were making good progress, and so far they had no problems. The girls found a spot between two trees to set up their makeshift tent. They placed the poles draped with buffalo skins against the direction of the wind. This created a barrier from the snow that was already starting to fall.

They built a small fire and wrapped themselves with fur skin blankets from their bed roll and laid down to rest. Reflections found they didn't need to speak aloud, the thoughts they shared was more than enough to keep each other company. The winter night raged on with howling winds that tore at the buffalo skins on their tent poles, leaving them flapping loose in the arctic breeze. The girls became frightened when they heard the cry of wolves through the blizzard of snow. They huddled closer together and covered their faces with the blankets leaving only a tiny hole for fresh air. Their warm breath heated the space they occupied, and made it more tolerable. Reflections agreed that they couldn't wait for the coming dawn.

Much to their dismay, dawn brought no safe haven. They awoke to find themselves hidden beneath blankets of snow. They couldn't see the sun through the dense whiteness that now canvassed the land. The storm hadn't passed yet, and if they stayed in their present location, they would become buried alive in the drifting snow.

Checking their direction again, they continued their journey southward through the raging storm. Their cheeks were frozen and their eyes stung from the coldness that enveloped their faces. The wind threw pelts of ice clad snow that clung to their clothing and layered them in ice from head to toe. It became so cold at one point in the late afternoon, that the girls had to cover their mouths because the air they breathed in was freezing their lungs.

When night fell upon them for the second day in their long journey, the girls sought refuge as fast as possible. The snow was deep now, almost past their knees. The girls spent the remainder of the second evening making snow shoes that they could attach to their rabbit fur boots. Satisfied with their work, they sat back to back and wrapped themselves up to settle in for another night of the arctic blast.

Dawn encroached on the softly slumbering girls. It brought with it the promises of a sunny day. The charcoal tinged clouds that floated across the red streaked sky gave a pleasant aura of peace as the girls ate the last of their provisions and strapped the crude snow shoes to their boots. Reflections noticed that each day of their journey seemed to get a little easier. They figured that one more day of travel was needed to reach the great river. After that, the village of In-Mut-Too-Yah Lat-Lat should only be a half a days walk from there.

Through out the day, the girls took the time to reflect on the events of the previous three days. They walked silently through the snow, often shaking their heads at one another in protest of what the other one thought. They were scared, and didn't know what the future held. All they could do is find this Chief and ask him what they should do about their village. They missed their mother terribly.

They longed to hear her speak their name twice, as she'd always done.

The night came faster than anticipated, and the girls reluctantly paused in their journey for another night. As they assembled their tent for the last time, they remarked to one another how sore they were. Reflections stated that "her legs had never been so sore." And her sister complained that she hadn't been able to "feel her toes" since the day before. Crabbily one girl laid out their bed rolls in the ice laden snow, while the other gathered wood for a fire. Tonight they decided they would try to find some rocks to warm in the fire and place at their feet.

As they laid together like they've done since their birth, this was the first time they went to bed with an empty belly. Their stomachs growling in anger of lack of food caused the girls to giggle and tee-hee over the noises emitted.

The fact that they could find humor in the moment was good change for their spirits.

The morning of the last day, the girls awoke with a renewed sense. They knew they were only a half a day away from the great river. As they packed their tent poles they spoke aloud that "tonight they would be in a warm lodge feasting on dried meats and cornbread." The thought of cornbread made Reflections stomach grumble, which promptly brought back the giggles they'd had the night before. Light hearted and travel weary the girls checked their direction and began the last day of their journey.

Long about midmorning their travel started in a downwards decent. They were coming out of the mountains and into the valley. Reflections was overjoyed when they spied the great river down below. They quickened their pace, for the thought of fresh water to drink was very appealing.

When they reached the icy bank of the great river, Reflections turned to her sister and spoke aloud;

"Sister, how are we to get across this icy water?"

"I don't know sister. The Great Spirit didn't tell us."

"Do you see a bridge nearby?"

"Well, I heard father speak of mighty land bridge that used to be here many lifetimes ago. But it was destroyed when the mountains became angry with one another."

"Let us sit for a spell. Maybe we can find some food somewhere. I cannot think anymore with my stomach making such noises."

"Okay sister, you find the wood and start a fire and I'll see if I can find us something to eat."

Reflections separated and went in search of their food and wood. The one sister's job was easy. Right away she found chunks of driftwood along the icy shore. The other sister was having quite a bit of trouble. She searched and searched but there was no food anywhere. And they could not fish the icy waters, as they couldn't take the life of any animal. Distraught, Reflections returned empty handed.

"I'm sorry my sister, I could not find us anything suitable to eat. I could find no plant shoots or berries. We are going to have to wait."

Contemplating their dilemma of crossing the river became the girls' first priority. A warm lodge and food awaited them not too far on the other side.

Warming themselves by the fire they tossed a few ideas back and forth and still came up with nothing. As each idea was thrown by the wayside, the girls' hopes lessened. Their once cheery spirits were now replaced with hopeless abandon.

Reflections rose and walked down to the icy bank. Frustration overcame her as she knelt and picked up a piece of discarded driftwood and threw it angrily in the water. Watching it sink and then bob back up to the surface and float effortlessly down the river made her leap for joy. Quickly she ran back up to her sister and told her what happened;
Sister! I have an idea! I know this will work! Let us shove this big piece of dried wood into the river and see if we can float on it!"

Reflections eyed her sister carefully and said;

"But how will be stop once we reach the other side?"

"Easy! We'll tuck a few pieces of wood inside our belts and use them as paddles! It HAS to work!"

For lack of a better option, Reflections went along with her sister's plan.

They gathered some rough looking wood and placed it inside their belts and then pushed with all their might and slid the huge dried log into the water. And just as her sister said, it floated! Carefully they positioned themselves on to the log. They fought hard to keep it from rolling beneath them. The icy water drenched their skirts and boots, chilling them instantly. Their lips chattered and their arms shook as they paddled with all their might into the fast moving current of the great river that separated the two pieces of land.

At first they thought their adventure to be an easy one when they reached the halfway point. But that quickly changed when a swell of the river tossed them up in the air and back down again. The girls screamed and fought the log some more. No matter how hard they tried, the log kept trying to flip them into the river.

Another swell came and this time they weren't as lucky, the log rolled and flung Reflections into the below freezing water. The other sister managed to hold on but heard her sister shriek in pain as the icy water assaulted her body.

Reflections barely caught her sister by the arm of her jacket, and towed her alongside the log. Within seconds her sister went unconscious from the freezing water. Reflections screamed and slapped her face trying to wake her from death. It was no use, if she didn't get her out of the water, she'd surely die.

Paddling with one arm, and holding on to her sister with the other, she maneuvered them within a few feet of the other side of the bank. Reflections jumped off the log and drug her sister to safety.

Reflections began tearing off her sisters layers of clothing and rubbing her blue and gray limbs. She grabbed her flints and started a quick fire and continued to rub the life back into her sister. Pulling the only partially dry blanket from her pack she swaddled her sister in it. Reflections sat with her sister in her lap and began sob and cry out to The Great Spirit;

"She cannot leave me great one! She is all I have! You cannot have her! It is not her time to go! If you have to take one, then you must take us both!"

The tears trailed down her cheeks and landed in her sister's hair. Her body was overcome with uncontrollable spasms as she continued to sob and hold her sister. Quite unexpectedly, a meek voice squelched her sobbing;

"Sister, you do not need to yell, I am right here."

Reflections hugged and kissed her sister, she'd never been so happy.

Tearfully she sputtered back;

"I am sorry I made you get on the log that was a bad idea."

"We made it didn't we?"

"Yes" her sister responded, "yes we did."

Unable to let go, Reflections held on to her sister for quite a while longer.

After their clothes dried, Reflections helped her sister get dressed and half carried her off the icy bank of the river. When they reached the tree line, she reached out and brushed the snow from a tree to make sure they were going in the right direction. Seeing her sister fight to keep walking pained her;

"Sister, please lean on my back and put your arms over my shoulders, I know I can carry you that way."

Her sister protested a bit, but when she was rested comfortably on her upon her sister's back, she promptly closed her eyes and drifted into unconsciousness. Reflections didn't care if she had to carry her sister the rest of the way, she'd get them to safety tonight!

Dredging through the snow Reflections was getting weaker and weaker.

They hadn't had any food for two days. She silently hoped In-Mut-Too-Yah Lat—Lat's village wasn't far away. She walked and walked, carrying her sister upon her back. The coming darkness began to worry her, for she needed to get her sister someplace warm or she'd die.

A short time later, Reflections heard the sound of crackling wood thrown on a hot fire. She could smell the smoke from the popping flames. Pretty soon she saw it, only about a hundred paces in front of her. With the last of her strength she staggered into a village of many Indians with her sister on her back.

When she reached the fire, Reflections fell to her knees in the snow, and slid her sister from her back. Mustering up what little she could, she pushed her sister next to the fire, and slipped into the darkness.

Nearby villagers rushed over to the girls, confused but sympathetic to their plight, they carried the girls into the lodge of their medicine man. When the women removed their frozen clothes, they discovered the unique oddity that these two women shared. Never before had any of them seen a miracle of birth such as this. These two women were alike in every way. They looked to be the same person, but there was two of them! The word spread quickly about these two strangers. It scared most of the inhabitants as they were unfamiliar with anything of this nature.

The women tended to the girls and the medicine man applied a greasy salve to their wind chapped faces. Slowly the girls' color returned to normal. The medicine man kept watch over the girls all through the night. He soothed them by stroking their hair when bouts of nightmares overtook them. They cried and mumbled in unison. The medicine man was in awe at how they could communicate even in their sleep.

The girls slept well into the next day. They awoke to find themselves dressed in warm furs and laying comfortably by a smoldering fire. Planks of dried salmon were laid within reaching distance. The girls hungrily chewed the flavorful pink flesh of the salmon and gulped the herbed water that was laid out before them. While they were eating, the girls remarked how lucky they were to be alive.

Reflections looked at her sister and motioned for her to stop chewing. She put down her tasty meal and spoke;

"My sister, I love you more than words can say. My spirit is overjoyed that I am sitting here enjoying a meal with you this day."

Reflections eyes grew misty and her voice became hoarse when she whispered back;

"As am I, thank you for saving me."

They continued their meal in silence, only sharing their thoughts between each other. When the last bite had been chewed and the last sip had been taken, the girls decided they'd better go in search of the person that so graciously had taken them in. Lifting the door of the round little lodge, they stepped out into the cold obnoxious air. Their faces stung when the wind blew towards them, causing them to wince in pain. They turned at the sound of a voice speaking to them;

"My heart is singing to see you, I am sorry I was not there when you awoke. I trust you are feeling better?"

"Yes, we are much better." (They answered in unison)

"Please come back inside my lodge, you should not be outside yet. I can tell the fever hasn't broken, you need more rest."

Reluctantly Reflections did as they were told. This kind old man reminded them of their father. The thought brought back the events that took place on their journey and they sadly sat down next to the fire. The old man was puzzled by the quick change in the girls' attitude, so he questioned them;

"Tell me young maidens, what has troubled you so?"

Reflections looked to each other and silently agreed who was going to speak of the tragedy that started with their very first journey. The old man knew they were communicating silently with each other, so he grabbed a small log from the nearby pile and placed it on the fire. He could tell by their hesitation that this must be a one that would be told with much pain and sorrow. Not wanting to rush them, he sat down and crossed his legs and dug himself in for their tale.

The girls began telling their fascinating tale, when one would become too emotional to continue, the other would pick up where she left off, not even missing a word. The old man was mesmerized by the uniqueness of the pair and at how they could alternate the story between them. Surely they must have been sent to him by The Great Spirit. The girls continued on long into the evening. The old man paid much attention to the details of their story, growing more concerned for them by the moment.

When they finished the tales of woe and hardship, the old man chewed on the end of his medicine pipe for a moment and cleared his throat. Giving the traditional pause before speaking he toyed with the edge of his sleeve before becoming the bearer of even more bad news.

"I heard you say you were in search of Chief In-Mut-Too-Yah Lat-Lat. Is that correct? If so, then you need look no further, I am he. I am the Chief of the Wal-Lam-Wat-Kin band of the Chute-Pa Lu. I am Chief In-Mut-Too-Yah Lat-Lat."

Excited by the old mans revelation, the girls began chattering excitedly to the old man and asking him the questions they needed answered. The old man raised his hands and said;

"Maidens, I cannot answer those questions for you. Those are answers you must find on your own. The only thing I can provide you with is the wisdom and truth that will guide you to them. I can tell your tribe has been far removed from the rest of the world. You are seeking answers that have already been answered with the passing of time. The only way for me to explain to you what has happened so that you can understand, is for me to start at the beginning. You are like the child that was thrown before the wolves."

Reflections answered;
"We don't understand what you say, what wolves do you speak of?"

"My innocent maidens, the white men are the wolves in which I speak of.

The white man may have more words than I to tell you how it looks to them, but for me, it does not require many words to speak the truth. What I have to say will come straight from my heart, and I will speak with a straight tongue. The Great Spirit is looking at me, and begs for you to hear me."

"The story is long, but it is only a testament of faith and strength of my people. You will be here a while, so I suggest you relax and try not to become upset at what you are about to learn."

More frightened than they could comprehend the girls adjusted their seating and focused on their speaker.

As you know, my name is In-Mut-Too-Yah Lat-Lat (Thunder Traveling Over Mountains). I was born here in the Oregon Territory Thirty-Eight winters ago. My father was chief before me. When he was a young man, he was called Joseph by Mr. Spaulding, a missionary white man. He died a few winters ago. He left a good name on earth. He advised me well for my people.

Our fathers gave us many laws, which they had learned from their fathers. These laws were good. They told us to treat all men as they treated us, that we should never break a bargain, that it was a disgrace to tell a lie, that we should speak only the truth, that it was a shame for one man to take from another his wife or his property without paying for it.

We were taught to believe that the Great Spirit sees and hears everything, and that He never forgets; that hereafter He will give every man a spirit home according to his deserts; If he was a good man, he will have a good home; If he has been a bad man, he will have a bad home.

This I believe and all my people believe the same. As I am sure yours believe.

We did not know there were other people besides us until about one hundred winters ago, when some men with white faces came to our country. They brought many things with them to trade for furs and skins. They brought tobacco, which was new to us. They brought guns with flint stones on them that frightened our women, and the children began calling them thunder sticks. Our people could not talk with these white-faced men, but they used signs which all people understand.

These men were called Frenchmen, and they called our people "Nez Perce," because some of them wore rings in their nose for ornaments. Although very few of our people wear them now, we are still called by the same name.

These French trappers said a great many things to our fathers, which have been planted in our hearts. Some were good for us, but some were bad.

Our people were divided in opinion about these men. Some thought they taught more bad than good. An Indian respects a brave man, but he despises a coward. He loves a straight tongue, but he hates a forked tongue. These French trappers told us some truths and some lies.

The next white men that came to our people were 2 men named Lewis and Clark. They also brought many things that our people had never seen. They talked straight, and our people gave them a great feast as proof that their hearts were friendly.

These men were very kind. They made presents to our chiefs and our people made presents to them. We had a great many horses, of which we gave them what they needed, and they gave us guns and tobacco in return.

All of the Nez Perce made friends with Lewis and Clark, and agreed to let them pass through their country, and never to make war on the white men. This promise the Nez Perce have never broken. No white man can accuse them of bad faith and speak with a straight tongue. It has always been the pride of my people that they were friends with the white man.

Before my father died, there came to our country a white man by the name of Rev. Henry H. Spaulding who talked spirit law. He won the affections of our people because he spoke good things to them. At first he did not say anything about white men wanting to settle on our lands. Nothing was said about that until a few winters ago, when a number of white people came into our country and built houses and made farms.

At first our people made no complaint. They thought there was room enough for all to live in peace, and they were learning many things from the white men that seemed to be good.

But we soon found that the white men were growing very rich very fast, and they were greedy to possess everything we had. My father was the first to see through the schemes of the white men, and he warned all the members of his tribe to be careful trading with them. He had suspicion of men who seemed anxious to make money. I remember well my father's caution. He had sharper eyes than the rest of my people.

Next there came a white officer by the name of Governor Isaac Stevens who invited all of my people to what he called a treaty council. After the council was opened, he made known his heart. He said there were a great many white people in our country, and many more would come; that he wanted the land marked out so that the Indians and the white men could be separated. If they were to live in peace it was necessary, he said, that the Indians should have a country set apart for them, and in that country we must stay.

My father, who represented his band, refused to have anything to do with the council, because he wished to be a free man. He claimed that no man owned any part of the earth, and a man could not sell what he did not own.

Mr. Spaulding took hold of my father's arm and said, "Come and sign the treaty."

My father pushed him away, and said, "Why do you ask me to sign away my country? It is your business to talk to us about spirit matters and not to talk to us about parting with our land."

Governor Stevens urged my father to sign his treaty, but he

refused. "I will not sign your paper," he said. "You go where you please, so do I. You are not a child. I am no child. I can think for myself. No man can think for me. I have no home other than this. I will not give it up to any man. My people would have no home. Take away your paper. I will not touch it with my hand."

My father left the council. Some of the chiefs of the other bands of the Nez Perce signed the treaty, and then Governor Stevens gave them presents of blankets. My father cautioned his people to take no presents, for "after a while,"

he said, "they will that you have accepted pay for your country."

My father was invited to many councils, and they tried hard to make him sign the treaty, but he was firm as the rock, and would not sign away his home. His refusal caused a difference among my people.

Soon at the next treaty council, a chief called lawyer, because he was a great talker, took the lead in the council, and sold nearly all the Nez Perce country.

My father was not there. He said to me; "When you go into council with the white man, always remember your country.

Do not give it away. The white man will cheat you out of your home. I have taken no pay from the United States. I have never sold our land."

In this treaty, Lawyer acted without authority from our band.

He had no right to sell the Wallowa country, which means "the land of winding water," It is in the northeastern part of what they call Oregon. This was the ancestral home of Joseph's band of the Nez Perce. It had always belonged to my father's own people, and other bands had never disputed our right to it. No other Indians ever claimed Wallowa.

In order to have all people understand how much land we owned, my father planted poles around it and said, "Inside is the home of my people. The white man may take the land outside. Inside this boundary all our people were. It circles around the graves of our fathers, and we will never give up these graves to any man."

The United States claimed they had bought all the Nez Perce country outside the Lapwai Reservation from Lawyer and other chiefs. But we continued to live on this land in peace until 2 winters ago, when white men began to come inside the boundaries my father had set.

We warned them against this great wrong, but they would not leave our land, and some bad blood was raised. The white men represented that we were going upon the warpath. They reported many things that were false.

The United States government again asked for a treaty council. My father had become blind and feeble. He could no longer speak for his people. It was then that I took my fathers place as chief. In this council I made my first speech to white men.

I said to the agent who held the council: "I did not want to come to this council, but I came hoping that we could save blood. The white man has no right to come here and take our country. We have never accepted any presents from the government. Neither Lawyer nor any other chief had authority to sell this land. It has always belonged to my people. It came unclouded to them from our fathers, and we will defend this land as long as a drop of Indian blood warms the hearts of our men."

The agent said he had orders from the Great White Chief at someplace called Washington for us to go upon a plot of land they called the Lapwai Reservation, and that if we obeyed, he would help us in many ways.

"You must move to the agency," he said.

I answered him, "I will not. I do not need your help. We have plenty, and we are contented and happy if the white man will let us alone. The reservation is too small for so many people with all their stock. You can keep your presents. We can go to your towns and pay for all we need. We have plenty of horses and cattle to sell, and we won't have any help from you. We are free now; we can go where we please. Our fathers were born here. Here they lived, and here they died, here are their graves. We will never leave them."

The agent went away and we had peace for a little while.

Soon after this my father sent for me. I saw he was dying. I took his hand in mine. He said, "My son, my body is returning to mother earth, and my spirit is going very soon to see the Great Spirit Chief. When I am gone, think of your country.

You are the chief of these people. They look to you to guide them. Always remember that your father never sold this country. You must stop your ears whenever you are asked to sign a treaty selling your home. A few years more, and white men will be all around you. They have their eyes on this land.

My son, never forget my dying words. This country holds your fathers body. Never sell the bones of your father and mother."

I pressed my father's hand and told him I would protect his grave with my life. My father smiled and passed away to the spirit land.

I buried him in that beautiful valley of the winding waters. I love that land more than all the rest of the world. A man who would not love his father's grave is worse than a wild animal.

For a short time we lived quietly. But this could not last.

White men found gold in the mountains around the land of winding water. They stole many horses from us, and we could not get them back because we were Indians.

The white men told lies for each other. They drove off a great many of our cattle. Some white men branded our young cattle so they could claim them.

We had no friend who would plead our cause before the law councils. It seemed to me that some of the white men in Wallowa were doing these things on purpose to get up a war.

They knew that we were not strong enough to fight them.

I labored hard to avoid trouble and bloodshed. We gave up some of our country to the white men, thinking that then we could have peace.

We were mistaken. The white man would not let us alone.

We could have avenged our wrongs many times, but we did not. Whenever the government had asked us to help them against other Indians, we never refused. When the white men were few and we were strong, we could have killed all of them off, but the Nez Perce wished to live at peace.

I believe the old treaty has never been correctly reported. If we ever owned the land we own it still, for we never sold it.

In the treaty councils the commissioners have claimed that our country had been sold to the government. Suppose a white man should come to me and say,

"Joseph, I like your horses, and I want to buy them."

I say to him, "No, my horses suit me. I will not sell them."

Then he goes to my neighbor and says to him, "Joseph has some good horses. I want to buy them, but he refuses to sell."

My neighbor answers, "Pay me the money, and I will sell you Joseph's horses."

The white man returns to me and says, "Joseph, I have bought your horses, and you must let me have them."

I say this girl's, if I sold my lands to the government, this is the way in which they were bought.

The girls were horrified beyond belief at what the chief was saying. They could not believe that the white man had grown to so many. And that they now referred to our country as the United States. How could this be? Eagerly they waited for more of Thunder Travelling over the Mountain's tale.

On account of the treaty made by other bands of the Nez Perce, the white men claimed my lands. We were troubled greatly by white men crowding over the line. Some of these were good men, and we lived on peaceful terms with them.

But they were not all good.

Nearly every month the agent came over from Lapwai and ordered us onto the reservation. We always replied that we were satisfied to live in Wallowa. We were careful to refuse presents or annuities which he offered.

Through all the years since the white men came to Wallowa,

We have been threatened and taunted by them and the treaty Nez Perce. They have given us no rest.

We had a few good friends among the white men, and they have always advised my people to bear these taunts without fighting. Our young men were quick tempered, and I have had great trouble in keeping them from doing rash things.

I have carried a heavy load on my back ever since I was a boy. I learned then that we were but few, while the white men were many, and that we could not hold our own with them.

We were like deer. They were like grizzly bears.

We had a small country. Their country was large.

We were contented to let things remain as the Great Spirit Chief made them. They were not, and would change the rivers and the mountains if they did not suit them.

Even after all their threats, no war was made upon my people until General Howard came to our country one year ago and told us he was the white war chief of all that country. He said, "I have a great many soldiers at my back.

I am going to bring them up here, and then I will talk to you again. I will not let white men laugh at me the next time I come. The country belongs to the government, and I intend to make you go upon the reservation."

I remonstrated with him against bringing more soldiers to

the Nez Perce country. He had one house full of troops all the time at Fort Lapwai.

The next spring the agent at Umatilla agency sent an Indian runner to tell me to meet General Howard at Walla Walla. I could not go myself, so I sent my brother and five other head men to meet him, and they had a long talk. General Howard said, "You have talked straight, and it is all right. You can stay in Wallowa."

He insisted that my brother go with him to Fort Lapwai. When the party arrived there General Howard sent out runners and called the Indians in to a grand council. I was in that council.

I said to General Howard, "We are ready to listen."

He answered that he would not talk then, but would hold a council the next day, when he would talk plainly.

I said to General Howard, "I am ready to talk today. I have been in great many councils, but I am no wiser. We are all sprung from a woman, although we are unlike in many things. We cannot be made over again. You are as you were made, and as you made you remain. We are just as we were made by the Great Spirit, and you cannot change us. Then why should children of one mother and one father quarrel?

Why should one try to cheat the other? I do not believe that the Great Spirit Chief gave one kind of men the right to tell another kind of men what they must do."

General Howard replied. "You deny my authority, do you?

You want to dictate to me, do you?"

Then one of my chiefs, Too-Hool-Hool Suit rose in the council and said to General Howard, "The Great Spirit Chief made the world as it is, and as He wanted it, and He made a part of it for us to live upon. I do not see where you get the authority to say that we shall not live where he placed us."

General Howard lost his temper and said, "Shut up! I don't want to hear anymore of such talk. The law says you shall go upon the reservation to live, and I want you to do so. But you persist in disobeying the law. If you do not move, I will take the matter into my own hand and make you suffer for your disobedience."

Too-Hool-Hool Suit answered, "Who are you, that you should ask us to talk, and then tell me I shan't talk? Are you the Great Spirit? Did you make the world? Did you make the sun? Did you make the rivers to run for us to drink? Did you make the grass to grow? Did you make all these things, that you talk to us as though we were boys? If you did, then you have the right to talk as you do."

General Howard sternly replied, "You are an impudent fellow, and I will put you in the guard house," and then he ordered a soldier to arrest him.

Too-Hool-Hool Suit made no resistance. He asked General Howard, "Is that your order? I don't care. I have expressed my heart to you . I have nothing to take back. I have spoken for my country. You can arrest me, but you cannot change me or make me take back what I have said."

The soldiers came forward and seized my friend and took him to the guard house. My men whispered among themselves whether they should let this thing be done.

I counseled them to submit. I knew if we resisted that all white men present, including General Howard, would be killed in a moment, and we would be blamed. If I had said nothing, General Howard would never have given another unjust order against my men.

I saw the danger, and while they dragged my friend to prison, I arose and said, "I am going to talk now. I don't care whether you arrest me or not."

I turned to my people and said, "The arrest of Too-Hool-Hool Suit was wrong, but we will not resent the insult. We were Invited to this council to express our hearts, and we have done so." They held my friend for five days before he was released.

The council broke up for that day. On the next morning, General Howard came to my lodge and invited me to go with him and White Bird and Looking Glass to look for a land for my people.

As we rode along we came to some good land that was already occupied by Indians and white people. General Howard, pointing to this land, said, "If you will come on to the reservation, I will give you these lands and move these people off."

I replied, "No. It would be wrong to disturb these people. I have no right to take their homes. I have never taken what did not belong to me. I will not now."

We rode all day upon the reservation, and found no good land unoccupied. I was informed by men who do not tell a lie that General Howard sent a letter that night telling the soldiers at Walla Walla to go to Wallowa valley and drive us out upon our return home.

In the council the next day, General Howard informed me, in a haughty spirit, that he would give my people thirty days to go back home, collect all their stock and move onto the reservation, saying , "If you are not here in that time, I shall consider that you want to fight, and will send my soldiers to drive you on.

I said, "War can be avoided, and it ought to be avoided. I want no war. My people have always been the friends of the white man. Why are you in such a hurry? I cannot get ready to move in thirty days. Our live stock is scattered and the Snake River is very high. Let us wait until fall. Then the river will be low. We want time to hunt up our stock and gather supplies for the winter."

General Howard replied, "If you let the time run over one day, the soldiers will be there to drive you onto the reservation, and all your cattle and horses outside of the reservation at that time will fall into the hands of the white men."

I knew I had never sold my country, and that I had no land here in Lapwai. But I did not want bloodshed. I did not want my people killed.

Some of my people had been murdered by white men, and the white murderers were never punished for it. I told General Howard about this, and again said I wanted no war.

I wanted the people who lived upon the lands I was to occupy here at Lapwai to have time to gather their harvest.

I said in my heart that, rather than have war, I would give up my country. I would give up my father's grave. I would give up everything rather than have the blood of white men upon the hands of my people.

General Howard refused to allow me more than thirty days to move my people and their stock. I am sure that he began to prepare for war at once.

When I returned home to Wallowa I found my people very much excited upon discovering that the soldiers were already in the Wallowa valley. We held a council and decided to move immediately, to avoid bloodshed.

Too-Hool-Hool Suit, who felt outraged by his imprisonment, talked for war, and made many of my young men willing to fight rather than be driven like dogs from the land where they were born. He declared that blood alone would wash out the disgrace General Howard had put upon him. It required a strong heart to stand up against such talk, but I urged my people to be quiet, and not begin a war.

We gathered all the stock we could find, and made an attempt to move. We left many of our horses and cattle in Wallowa, and we lost several hundred in crossing the river.

All of my people succeeded in getting across safely.

Many of the Nez Perce came together in Rocky Canyon to hold a grand council. I went with all my people. This council lasted ten days. There was a great deal of war talk, and a great deal of excitement. There was one young brave present whose father had been killed by a white man five years before. This man's blood was bad against the white men, and he left the council calling for revenge.

Again I counseled peace, and I thought the danger was past.

We had not complied with General Howard's order because we could not, but we intended to do so as soon as possible. I was leaving the council to kill beef for my family when the news came that the young man whose father had been killed had gone out with several other hot blooded young braves and killed four white men.

He rode up to the council and shouted, "Why do you sit here like women? The war has begun already."

I was deeply grieved. All the lodges were moved except my brother's and my own. I saw clearly that the war was upon us when I learned that my young men had been secretly buying ammunition. I heard then that Too-Hool-Hool Suit , who had been imprisoned by General Howard, had succeeded in organizing a war party.

I knew their acts would involve all of my people. I saw that the war could not be prevented. The time had passed.

I counseled peace from the beginning. I knew that we were too weak to fight the United States. We had many grievances, but I knew that war would bring more.

We had good white friends, who advised us against taking the war path. My friend and brother, Mr. Chapman, who has been with us since the surrender, told us just how the war would end. Mr. Chapman took sides against us, and helped General Howard. I do not blame him for doing so. He tried hard to prevent bloodshed.

We hoped the white settlers would not join the soldiers.

Before the war commenced we had discussed this matter all over, and many of my people were in favor of warning them that if they took no part against us they should not be molested in the event of war being begun by General Howard.

This plan was voted down in the war council.

There were bad men among my people who had quarreled with the white men, and they talked of their wrongs until they roused all the bad hearts in the council. Still, I could not believe they would begin the war.

I know that my young men did a great wrong, but I ask, "Who was first to blame?" They had been insulted a thousand times. Their fathers and brothers had been killed. Their mothers and wives had been disgraced. They had been driven to madness by whiskey sold to them by white men.

They had been told by General Howard that all their horses and cattle which they had been unable to drive out of Wallowa were to fall into the hands of white men. And, added to all this, they were homeless and desperate.

I would have given my own life if I could have undone the killing of white men by my people.

I blame my young men and I blame the white men. I blame General Howard for not giving my people time to get their stock away from Wallowa. I do not acknowledge that he had the right to order me to leave Wallowa at any time. I deny that either my father or myself ever sold that land. It is still our land. It may never again be my home, but my father sleeps there, and I love it as I love my mother. I left there hoping to avoid bloodshed.

If General Howard had given me plenty of time to gather up my stock, and treated Too-Hool-Hool Suit as a man should be treated, there would have been no war.

My friends among white men have blamed me for the war. I am not to blame. When my young men began the killing, my heart was hurt. Although I did not justify them, I remembered all the insults I had endured, and my blood was on fire. Still,

I would have taken my people to the buffalo country without fighting if possible. I could see no other way to avoid a war.

We moved over to White Bird Creek, sixteen miles away, and there encamped, intending to collect our stock before leaving. But the soldiers attacked us, and the first battle was fought.

We numbered in that battle sixty men, and the soldiers a hundred. The fight lasted but a few minutes, when the soldiers retreated before us for twelve miles. They lost thirty—three killed, and had seven wounded.

When we fight, we only shoot to kill. But soldiers shoot at random. None of the soldiers were scalped. We do not believe in scalping, nor in killing wounded men. Soldiers do not kill many of us unless they are wounded and left upon the battle field. Then they kill us.

Seven days after the first battle, General Howard arrived in the Nez Perce country, bringing seven hundred more soldiers. It was now war in earnest.

We crossed the Salmon River, hoping General Howard would follow. We were not disappointed. He did follow us, and we got back between him and his supplies, and cut him off for three days.

He sent out two companies to open the way. We attacked them, killing one officer, two guides, and ten men.

We withdrew, hoping the soldiers would not follow. But

they had got enough fighting for that day. They entrenched themselves, and the next day we attacked them again. The battle lasted all day, and was renewed next morning. We killed four and wounded seven or eight.

About this time General Howard found out that we were in his rear. Five days later he attacked us with three hundred and fifty soldiers and settlers. We had two hundred and fifty warriors.

The fight lasted twenty seven hours. We lost four killed and several wounded. General Howard's loss was twenty nine men killed and sixty wounded.

The following day the soldiers charged upon us, and we retreated with our families and stock a few miles, leaving eighty lodges to fall into General Howard's hands.

Finding that we were outnumbered, we retreated to the Bitterroot valley. Here another body of soldiers came upon us and demanded our surrender.

We refused.

They said, "You cannot get by us."

We answered, "We are going by you without fighting if you let us. But we are going by you anyhow."

We then made a treaty with these soldiers. We agreed not to molest anyone, and they agreed that we might pass through the Bitterroot country in peace.

We bought provisions and traded stock with the white men there.

We understood that there was to be no more war. We intended to go peaceably to the buffalo country, and leave the question of returning to our country to be settled afterward.

With this understanding, we traveled on for four days. And thinking that the trouble was all over, we stopped and prepared tent poles to take with us.

We started again, and at the end of two days saw three white men passing our camp. Thinking that peace had been made, we did not molest them. We could have killed them or taken them prisoners, but we did not suspect them of being spies, which they were.

That night the soldiers surrounded our camp. About daybreak one of my men went out to look after his horses.

The soldiers saw him and shot him down like a coyote.

I have since learned that these soldiers were not those we left behind. They had come upon us from another direction.

The new white war chief's name was Gibbon. He charged upon us while some of my people were still asleep. We had a hard fight. Some of my men crept around and attacked the soldiers from the rear. In this battle, we nearly lost all our lodges, but we finally drove General Gibbon back.

Finding that he was not able to capture us, he sent to his camp a few miles away for his big guns. (cannons) But my men captured them and all their ammunition.

We damaged the big guns all we could, and carried away all the powder and the lead.

In the fight with General Gibbon we lost fifty women and children and thirty fighting men. We remained long enough to bury our dead. The Nez Perce never make war on women and children. We could have killed a great many women and children while the war lasted, but we would feel ashamed to do so cowardly an act.

You know we never scalp our enemies. But when General Howard came up and joined General Gibbon, their Indian scouts dug up our dead and scalped them. I have been told that General Howard did not order this great shame to be done.

We retreated as rapidly as we could toward the buffalo country. After six days General Howard came close to us, and we went out and attacked him, and captured nearly all of his horses and mules. We then marched on to the Yellowstone Basin.

On the way we captured one white man and two white women. We released them at the end of three days. They were treated kindly. The women were not insulted. No white soldier could ever tell of a time when Indian women were taken prisoner and held three days and released without being insulted. The Nez Perce women who fell into the hands of General Howard's soldiers were not treated with much respect.

A few days later we captured two more white men. One of them stole a horse and escaped. We gave the other a poor horse and told him he was free.

Nine days' march brought us to the mouth of Clark's Fork of the Yellowstone. We did not know what had become of General Howard, but we supposed that he had sent for more horses and mules.

He did not come up, but another new war chief (General Sturgis) attacked us. We held him in check while we moved all our women and children and stock out of danger, leaving a few men to cover our retreat.

Several days passed, and we heard nothing of General Howard, or Gibbon, or Sturgis. We had repulsed each in turn, and began to feel secure, when another army, under General Miles, struck us. This was the fourth army, each of which outnumbered our fighting force that we had encountered within sixty days.

We had no knowledge of General Miles's army until a short time before he made a charge upon us, cutting our camp in two and capturing nearly all our horses.

About seventy men, including myself among them, were cut off. My little daughter, twelve years old, was with me. I gave her a rope and told her to catch a horse and join the others who were cut off from camp. I have not seen her since, but I have learned that she is alive and well.

I thought of my wife and children who were now surrounded by soldiers, and I resolved to go to them or die.

With a prayer in my mouth to the Great Spirit Chief who rules above, I dashed unarmed through the line of soldiers. It seemed to me that there were guns on every side, before and behind me.

My clothes were cut to pieces and my horse was wounded, but I was unharmed. As I reached the door of my lodge, my wife handed me my rifle, saying, "Here's your gun. FIGHT!"

The soldiers kept up a continuous fire.

Six of my men were killed in one spot near me. Ten or twelve soldiers charged into our camp and got possession of two lodges, killing three Nez Perce and losing three of their men who fell inside our lines.

I called my men to drive them back.

We fought at close range, not more than twenty steps apart, and drove the soldiers back upon their main line, leaving their dead in our hands.

We secured their arms and ammunition. We lost the first day and night, eighteen men and three women. General Miles lost twenty six killed and forty wounded.

The following day General Miles sent a messenger into my camp under protection of the white flag. I sent my friend Yellow Bull to meet him.

Yellow Bull understood the messenger to say that General Miles wished me to consider the situation, that he did not want to kill my people unnecessarily. Yellow Bull understood this to be a demand for me to surrender and save blood.

Upon reporting this message to me, Yellow Bull said he wondered whether General Miles was in earnest. I sent him back my answer that I had made up my own mind, but would think about it and send word soon.

A little later he sent some Cheyenne scouts with another message. I went out to meet them.

They said they believe General Miles was sincere and really wanted peace.

I walked to General Miles's tent. He met me and we shook hands. He said, "Come, let us sit down by the fire and talk this matter over."

I remained with him all night. The next morning, Yellow Bull came over to see if I was alive, and why I did not return.

General Miles would not let me leave the tent to see my friend alone.

Yellow Bull said to me, "They have got you in their power, and I am afraid they will never let you go again. I have an officer in our camp, and I will hold him until they let you go free."

I said, "I do not know what they mean to do with me, but if they kill me you must not kill the officer. It will do no good to avenge my death by killing him."

Yellow Bull returned to my camp.

I did not make any agreement that day with General Miles. The battle was renewed while I was with him. I was very anxious about my people. I knew that we were near Sitting Bull's camp in King George's land, and I thought maybe the Nez Perce who had escaped would return with assistance.

No great damage was done to either party during the night.

On the following morning I returned to my camp by agreement, meeting the officer who had been held a prisoner in my camp at the flag of truce.

My people were divided about surrendering. We could have escaped from Bear Paw Mountain if we had left our wounded, old men, and children behind. We were unwilling to do this. We had never heard of a wounded Indian recovering while in the hands of white men.

On the evening of the fourth day, General Howard came in with a small escort, together with my friend Chapman. We could now talk understandingly.

General Miles said to me in plain words, "If you will come out and give up your arms, I will spare your lives and send you to your reservation." I do not know what passed between General Miles and General Howard.

I could no longer bear to see my wounded men and women suffer any longer. We had lost enough already.

General Miles had promised that we might return to our own country with what stock we had left. I thought we could start again. I believe General Miles, or I never would have surrendered.

I had heard that he had been censured for making the promise to return us to Lapwai. He could not have made any other terms with me at the time. I would have held him in check until my friends came to my assistance, and then neither of the generals nor their soldiers would have ever left Bear Paw Mountain alive.

On the fifth day I went to General Miles and gave up my gun, and said, "I will fight no more."

My people needed rest. We wanted peace.

I was told we could go with General Miles to Tongue River and stay there until spring, when we would be sent back to our country.

Finally it was decided that we were about to be taken to Tongue River. We had nothing to say about it. After our arrival at Tongue River, General Miles received orders to take us to Bismarck. The reason given was that subsistence would be cheaper there.

General Miles opposed this order. He said, "You must

not blame me. I have endeavored to keep my word, but the chief who is over me has given the order, and I must obey it or resign. That would do no good. Some other officer would carry out the order."

I believe General Miles would have kept his word if he could have done so. I do not blame him for what we have suffered since the surrender. I do not know who is to blame. We gave up all our horses, over eleven hundred, and all of our saddles, over one hundred. And we have not heard from them since. Someone has got our horses.

General Miles turned my people over to another soldier, and we were taken to Bismarck.

Captain Johnson, who now had charge of us, received an order to take us to Leavenworth. At Leavenworth we were placed on a low river bottom, with no water except river water to drink and cook with.

We had always lived in a healthy country, where the mountains were high and the water was cold and clear.

Many of my people sickened and died, and we buried them in that strange land.

I cannot tell you how much my heart suffered for my people while at Leavenworth. The Great Spirit Chief who rules above seemed to be looking the other way, and did not see what was being done to my people.

During the hot days we received notice that we were to be

moved farther away from our own country. We were not asked if we were willing to go.

We were ordered to get into railroad cars. Three of my people died on the way to Baxter Springs. It was worse to die there than to die fighting in the mountains.

We were moved from Baxter Springs to the Indian Territory, and set down without lodges. We had but little medicine, and we were nearly all sick.

Seventy of my people died since we moved there.

We had a great many visitors who have talked many ways.

Some of the chiefs from Washington came to see us, and selected land for us to live upon. We could not move to that land, for it was not a good place to live.

The commissioner, Chief Hayt came to see us. I told him, as I told everyone, that I expected General Miles's word would be carried out.

He said it could not be done, that the white men now lived in my country and all the land was taken up; that if I returned to Wallowa, I could not live in peace; that law-papers were out against my young men who began the war; and that the government could not protect my people.

This talk fell like a heavy stone upon my heart.

I saw that I could not gain anything by talking to him. Other law chiefs then came to see me and said they would help me get a healthy country.

I did not know who to believe. The white men have too many chiefs. They do not understand each other. They do not talk alike.

The Commissioner Chief invited me to go with him and hunt for a better home than we had. I liked the land we found west of the Osage Reservation better than any place I have seen in their country.

But it was not healthy land. There were no mountains or rivers. The water was warm, and it wasn't good country for stock.

I did not believe my people could live there, for I was afraid they would all die. The Indians who occupied that country were all dying off. I promised Chief Hayt to go there and do the best I could until the government got ready to make good on General Miles's word. I was not satisfied, but I could not help myself.

Then an inspector Chief General McNeill came to my camp and we had a long talk. He said I ought to have a home in the mountain country north, and that he would write a letter to the Great Chief in Washington. Again the hope of seeing the mountains of my home grew up in my heart.

At last I was granted to permission to come to travel to my homelands. We gathered what little people were left and they put us back in box cars and shipped us back out west. None of my people died on the journey home, for they lived for the thought of seeing our homeland one last time.

"Today my dear maidens, I am still far from my ancestral home. They placed us upon this ground and said we mustn't leave. We cannot go into the nearest town and buy goods or supplies. And when I think of our condition here my heart is heavy. I see men of my race treated as outlaws and driven away, or shot down like animals."

"We asked the white men to be recognized as men. We asked them that the same law shall work alike on all men. Let us be free men, free to travel, free to stop, free to work, free to trade when I choose, free to choose my own teachers, free to follow the religion of my fathers, free to think and talk and act for myself."

"But they will not grant this. We have no choice but to do what they tell us to do. They have stolen our country and have no desire to return it. I thank you for the time you spent listening to an old man's tale. But I felt it was an important one to tell you. The war is over and has been, we lost a battle we didn't even know we were fighting until it was too late."

"Your tribe lived far up into the mountains where only very few brave white men dared to venture. You had no idea what has happened. There is no chance at fighting these white men. They have killed off over eighty percent of us. To them, we are now just a handful of pebbles scattered amongst the boulders."

Reflections just sat and stared at the old man before them.

The realization that their entire country was now overrun by the white man was an unimaginable possibility. But yet they have sat here in his lodge for the entire evening listening to his story. What he says must be true. The girls realized at that moment that this was what their father was talking about. He had said that what he knew he couldn't tell us.

Thunder Traveling over the Mountains interrupted the girls silent thoughts;

"If you care for anyone that is left at your village, I suggest that you get back to them as soon as possible. I have had many dealings with Governor Isaac Stevens, and it won't be long before he takes what is left of this country and buries it beneath the feet of the white man."

"I caution you two if you do decide to go, for no Indians are allowed off the reservation in this area, and if you are caught by white soldiers you will surely have your bodies insulted while in captivity. You need to travel by night fall until you reach the Great River. Once on the other side, you should be safer, for that is not their territory yet."

Numbly the girls looked blankly down at their feet. They came here seeking a purpose only to find that once they arrived, it was futile. They needed to leave as soon they could, they were not going to let their mother fall into the hands of those murderous creatures. They had to find a safe place for all of them to go. But where? The old man already told them the whole country was invaded.

Unsure of what they needed to do, Reflections asked the old man if they could borrow his lodge for a few minutes of prayer. The girls felt they needed some guidance. The old man graciously agreed and exited his home.

Sitting cross legged in front of each other, the girls matched their palms together and interlaced their fingers. Silently they agreed to speak the ancient chant meant to summon the Great Spirit.

Of mother earth and father sky, from mighty sun to sister moon, from the east, south, west and north, I call upon brother wind. Gentle as the summer breeze and as strong as the winter storms. Breathe upon us the insight of The Great Spirit, for we are they that walked before us. We are the same as a drop of rain or the majestic mountain, for what once was, shall be again!

The old man decided to check on the girls when he heard what sounded like many whispering voices coming from within the lodge. Gingerly he lifted the door of his lodge only to find the two identical maidens bathed in the most beautiful blue light he'd ever seen. The wind started to pick up inside his lodge like it was out in the open prairie. Suddenly he found himself being flung from the door of his lodge like a leaf blowing in the wind.

Not knowing what to do, the old man laid there in the snow watching the fantastic light show seeping through the cracks in his lodge. Then as quickly as it had started, it stopped. Timidly he crept to the entrance of his lodge, and very carefully he lifted only the very corner of the flap. What he saw taking place inside his lodge made him want to sing praises to The Great Spirit, for only He could have done this…

Look for the answers in book two, coming soon!

RESOURCES

The wisdom of the Native Americans
By: Kent Nerburn
Published by: MJF Books,
Fine communications
322 Eighth Ave.
New York, NY
10001

Chief Seattle's Public Speech given to governor Isaac Stevens, in December, 1853 on the shores of the Whulge
Transcribed by: Dr. Henry Smith

Chief Joseph's Public Speech given on January 14th, 1879 at Lincoln Hall in Washington D.C.

Wikipedia.com